The Art of Baseball: Book of Cartoons

Featuring Cartoons From
Barron's
The New Yorker
The Wall Street Journal
and more!

Front Cover illustration: Danny Shanahan
Back Cover illustration: Pat Brynes
Introduction: Bob Mankoff
Book Design: Darren Kornblut

Dedicated to Dan Kornblut who loved the Giants,
Jennifer & Bea

Cartoon Collections, LLC
10 Grand Central, 29th Floor
New York, NY 10017

For cartoon licensing information visit www.cartoonstock.com

First edition published 2023

ISBN: 978-1-963079-05-0 / Item # 46497

Introduction

Greetings baseball fans! Bob Mankoff here, former Cartoon Editor of *The New Yorker*, and it's my pleasure to introduce you to "The Art of Baseball Cartoons" Book!

As a lifelong fan of the game, I've always appreciated the humor that can be found both on and off the field. Whether it's a clever quip from a player or a humorous take on the game in a cartoon, there's no shortage of laughs to be had when it comes to America's favorite pastime.

Now, I know what you might be thinking. "Bob, how can a book of cartoons about baseball be funny?" Well, let me tell you, my friend, baseball is a sport that has been satirized and caricatured for as long as it has been played. From the earliest days of political cartoons to the modern era of internet memes, baseball has always been a rich source of comedic material. These cartoons offer a fresh perspective on the game we all love.

But it's not just the game itself that makes these cartoons so hilarious. It's the larger-than-life personalities of the players, coaches, and fans.

So, whether you're a baseball fanatic or just someone looking for a good laugh, this book has got you covered. It's a home run of humor, a fastball of fun, and a hit out of the park of hilarity. So, sit back, relax, and get ready to laugh your way through nine innings of comedic gold.

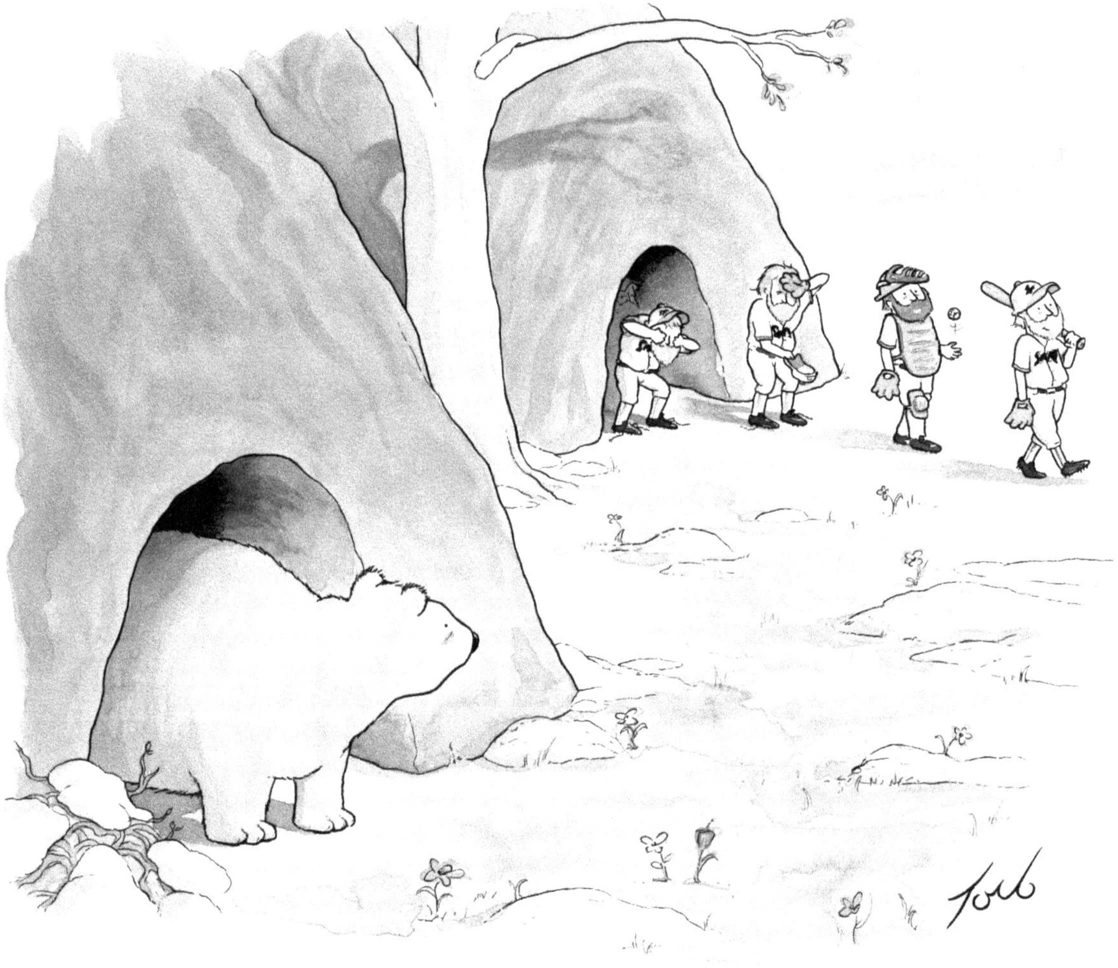

"Sure, I'm a fan but I don't think I'm rabid."

SPRING TRAINING

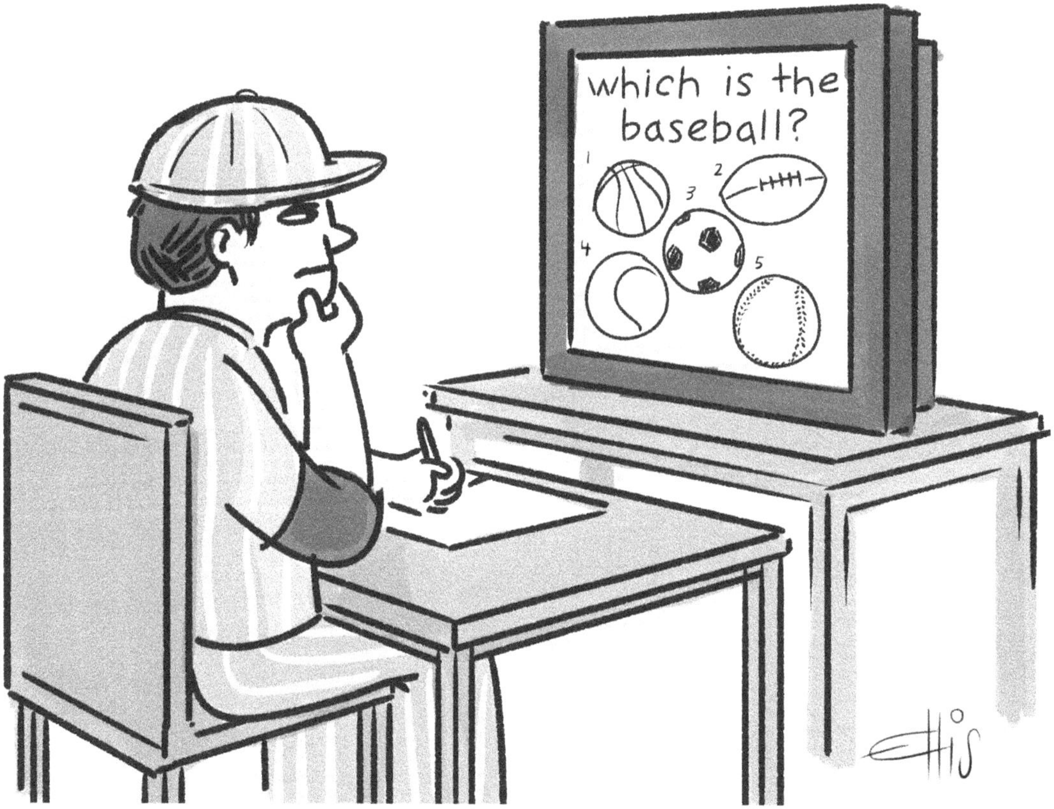
which is the baseball?
1
2
3
4
5

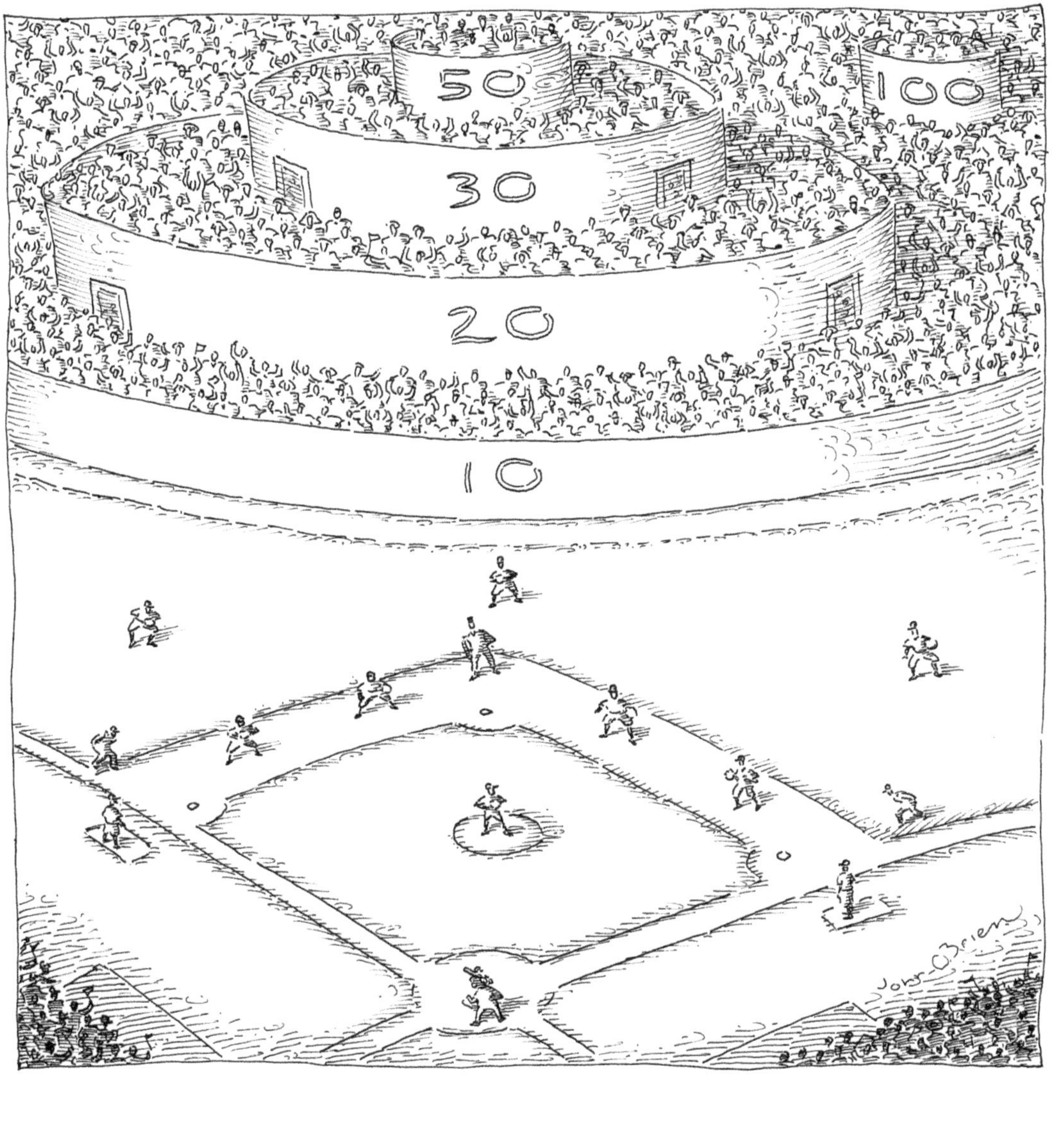
50
100
30
20
10
John O'Brien

"Life has its seasons, Kaitlin. This is baseball season."

"We're offering twenty million plus incentives over a four-year period, Mrs. Morton. Can Timmy come out and play?"

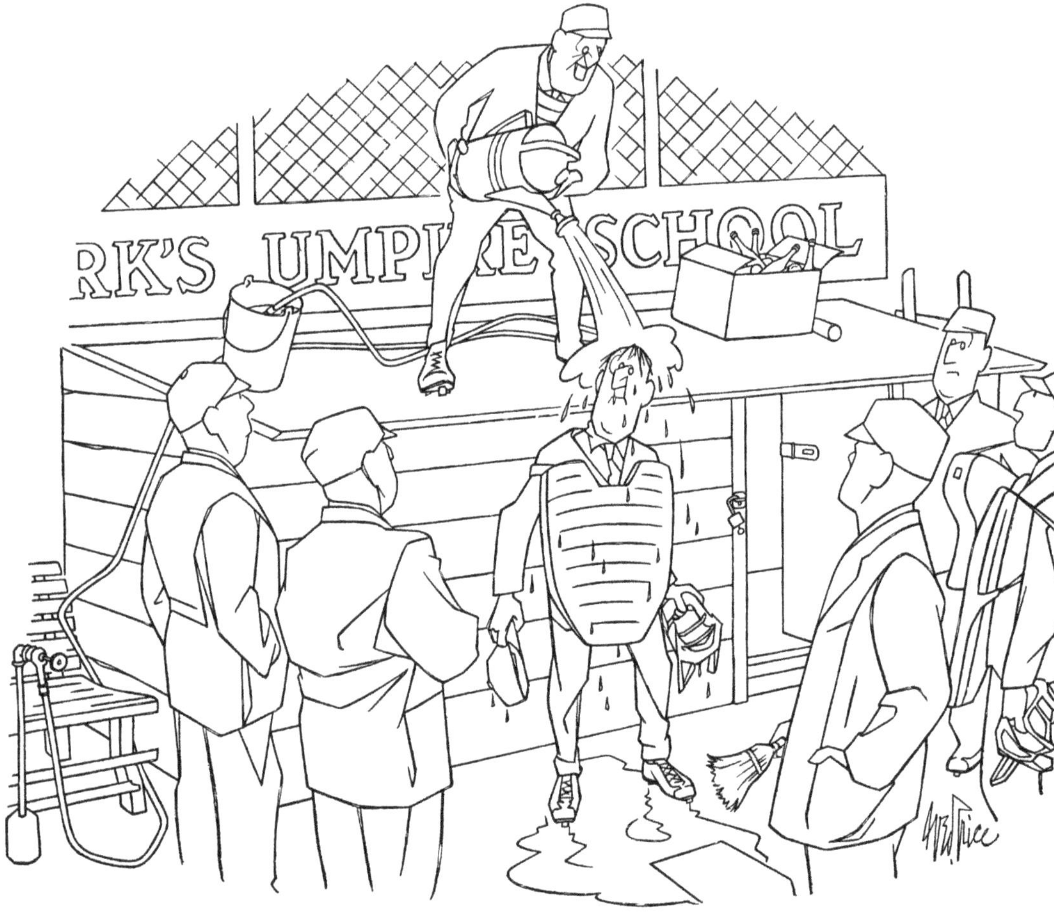
RK'S UMPIRE SCHOOL

*"All right, it's starting to come a little heavier.
Now will you call the game?"*

1 B
2 B
3 B
MANKOFF

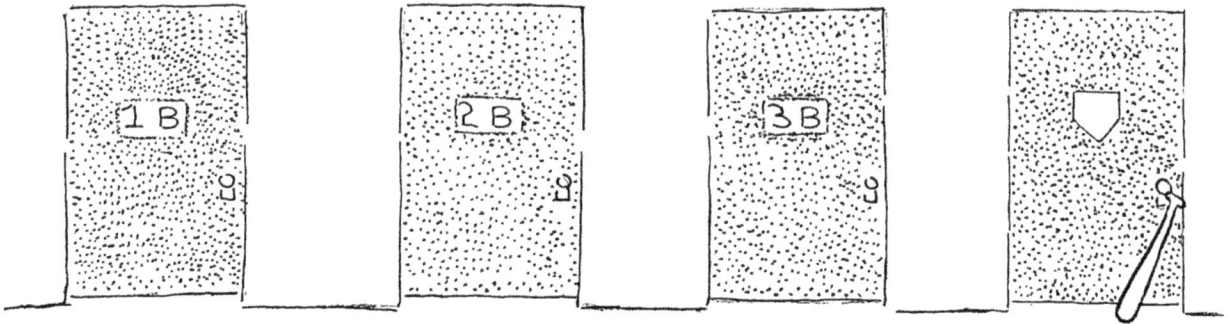

"Seriously, fellas, I can't get up."

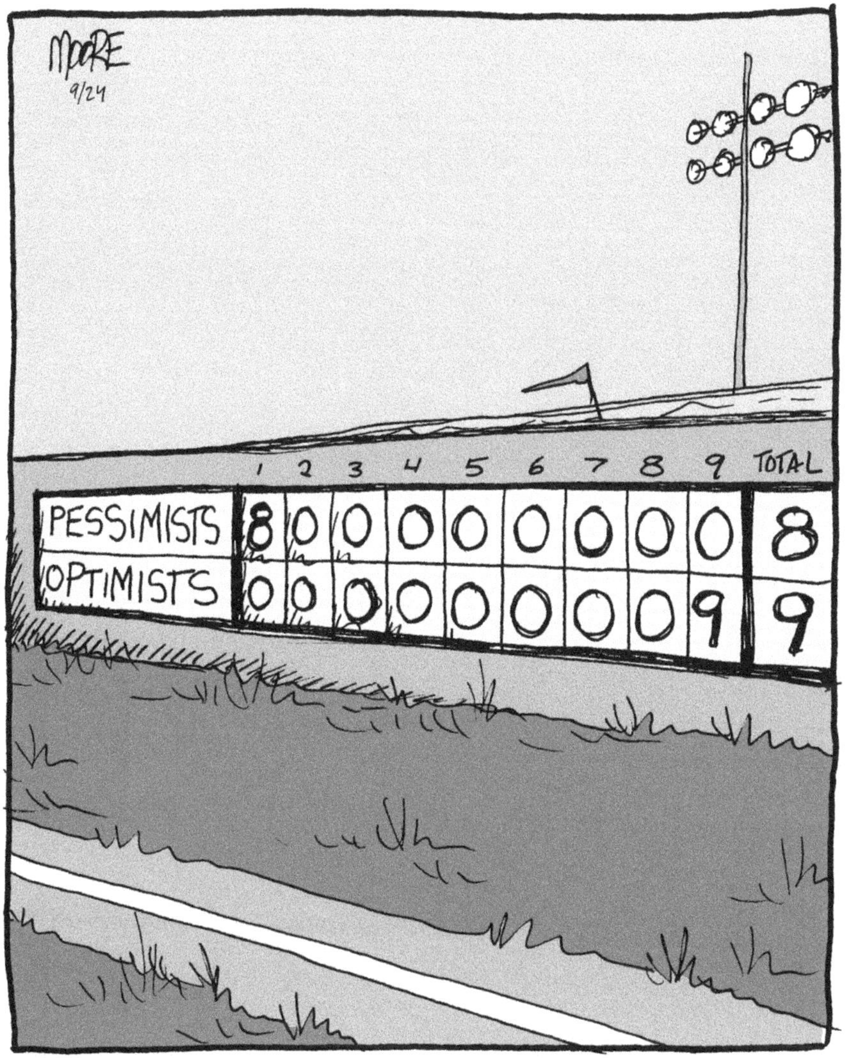
MOORE
9/24
1 2 3 4 5 6 7 8 9 TOTAL
PESSIMISTS 8 0 0 0 0 0 0 0 0 8
OPTIMISTS 0 0 0 0 0 0 0 0 9 9

"Poor Henry – he never returned from the All-Star break."

"*Are there any here today who feel this union is not in the best interests of baseball?*"

"*Anybody up there need an autograph?*"

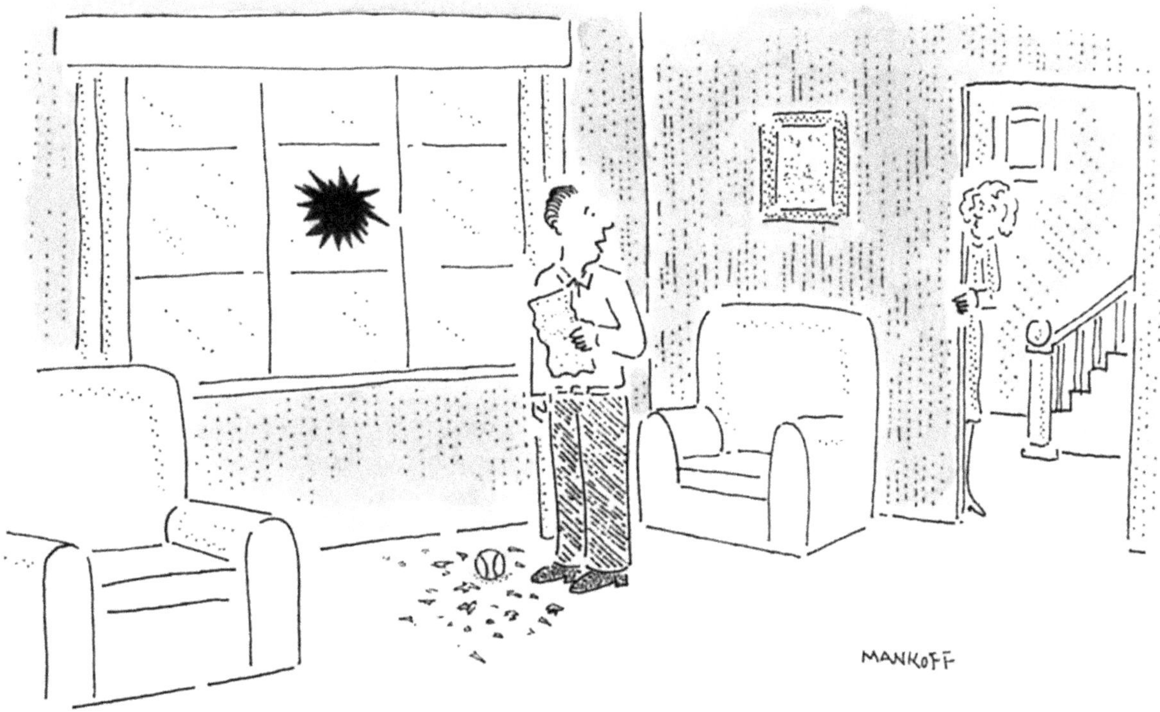
MANKOFF

"Why, it's a message from Major League Baseball."

"Of course I'm paying attention—I've pressed the mute button."

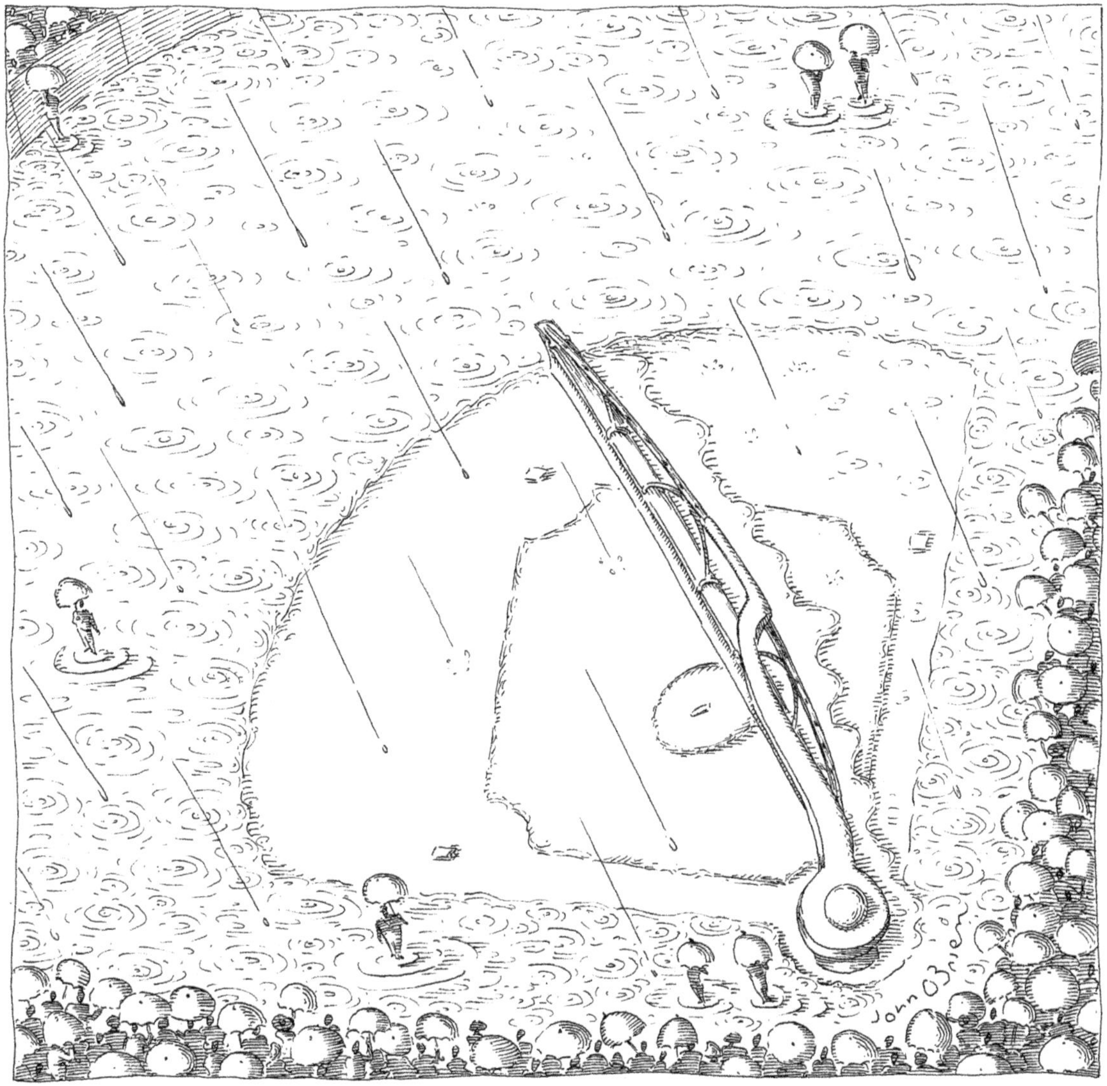

"Gimme a hand—I'm stuck."

"Look, I know you think you've got the stuff, but I'm telling you: walk God."

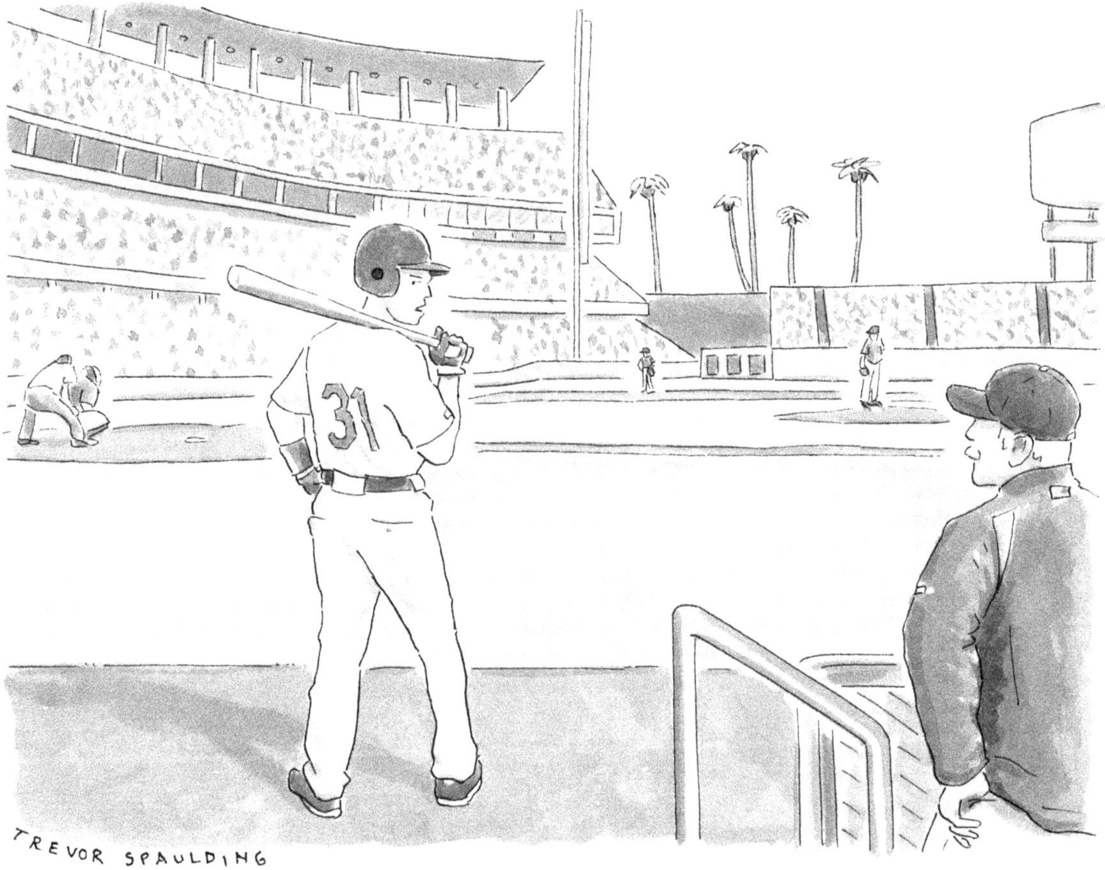
31
TREVOR SPAULDING

"Did you really just tell me to keep my eye on the ball?"

P.BYRNES.

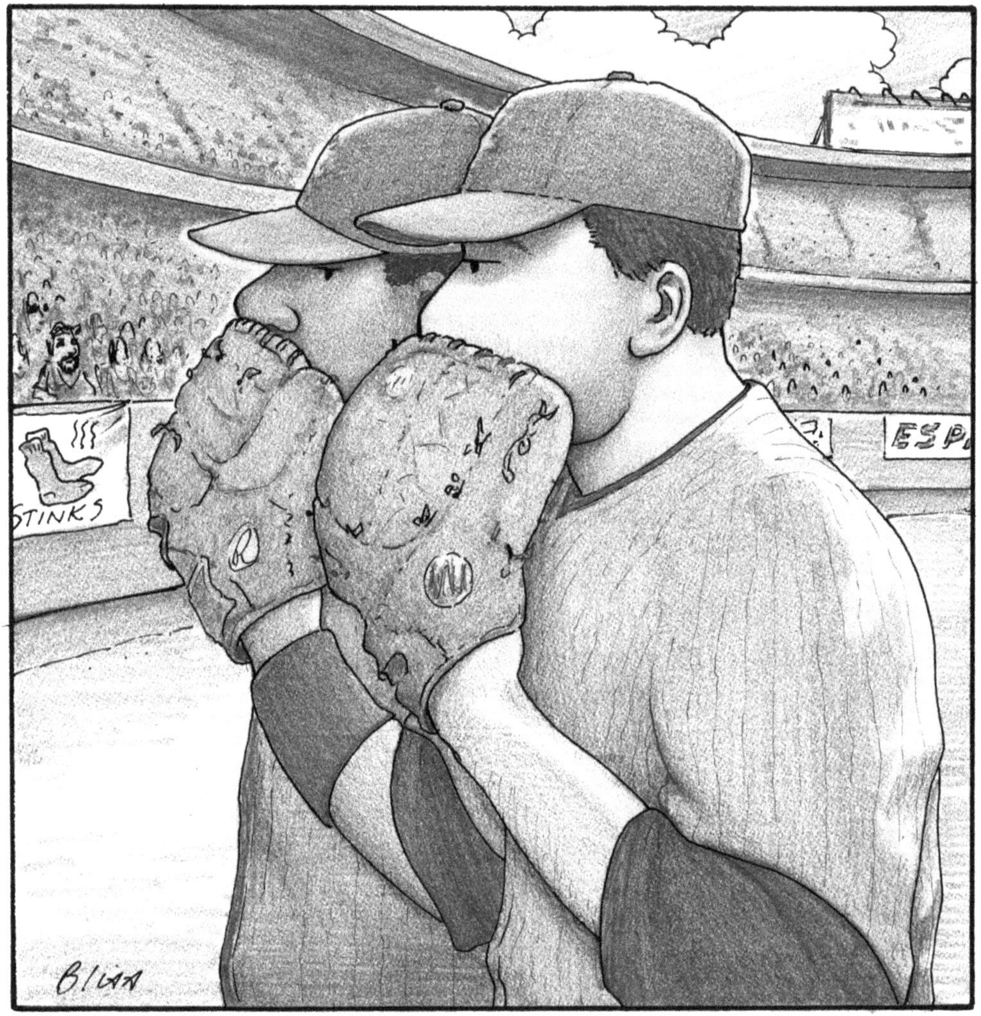
STINKS
ESP

"Well, there's your problem right there—you need to sauté the onions in white wine before adding the ginger."

"Roy, if you can hear me, the Mets are twenty games over .500 and
they have a good shot at clinching the N. L. East."

"This is a nice restaurant. Turn your cap around."

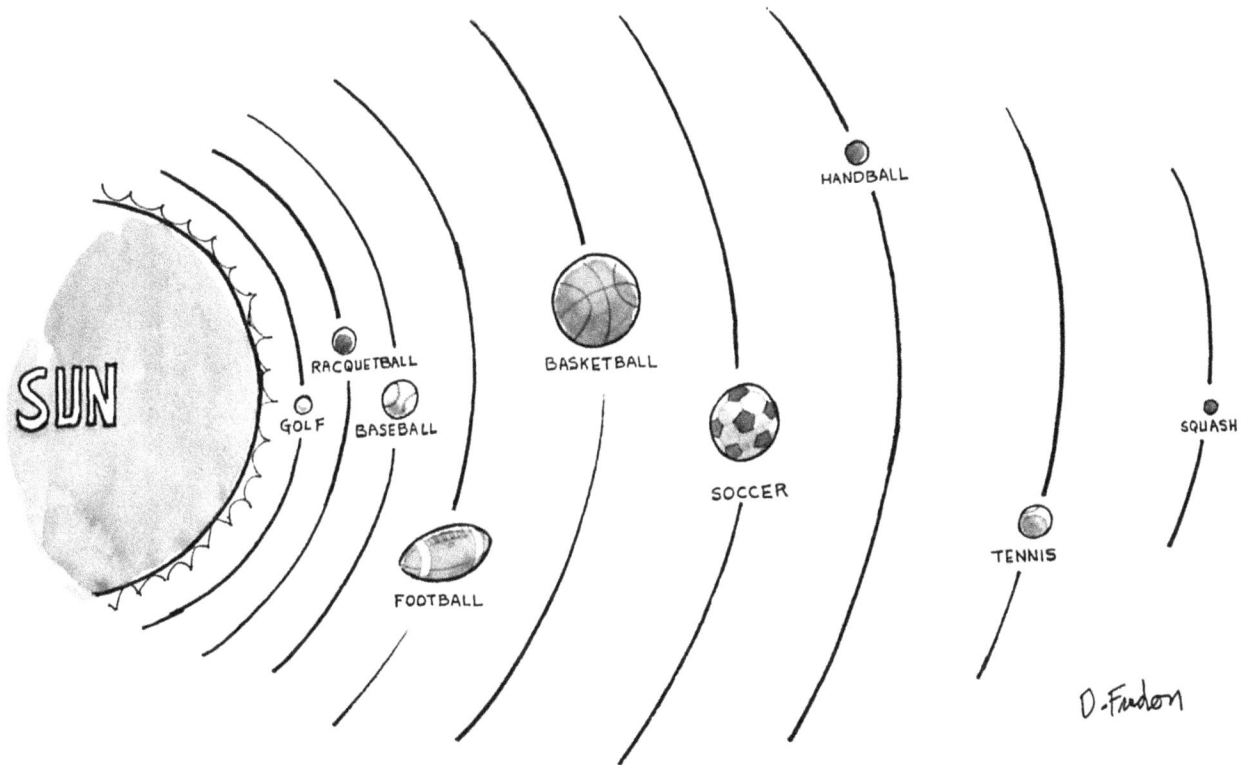

SUN

GOLF

RACQUETBALL

BASEBALL

FOOTBALL

BASKETBALL

SOCCER

HANDBALL

TENNIS

SQUASH

D.-Fradon

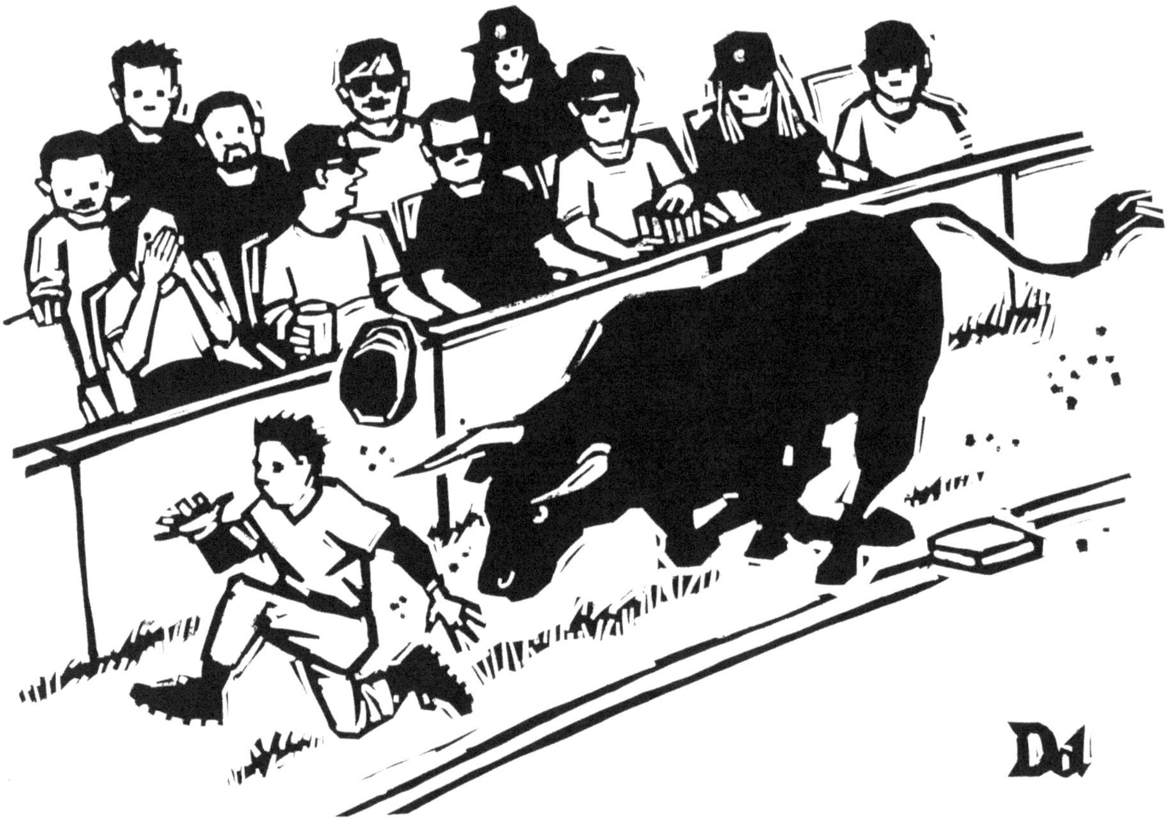
Dd

"This speeds up the game significantly."

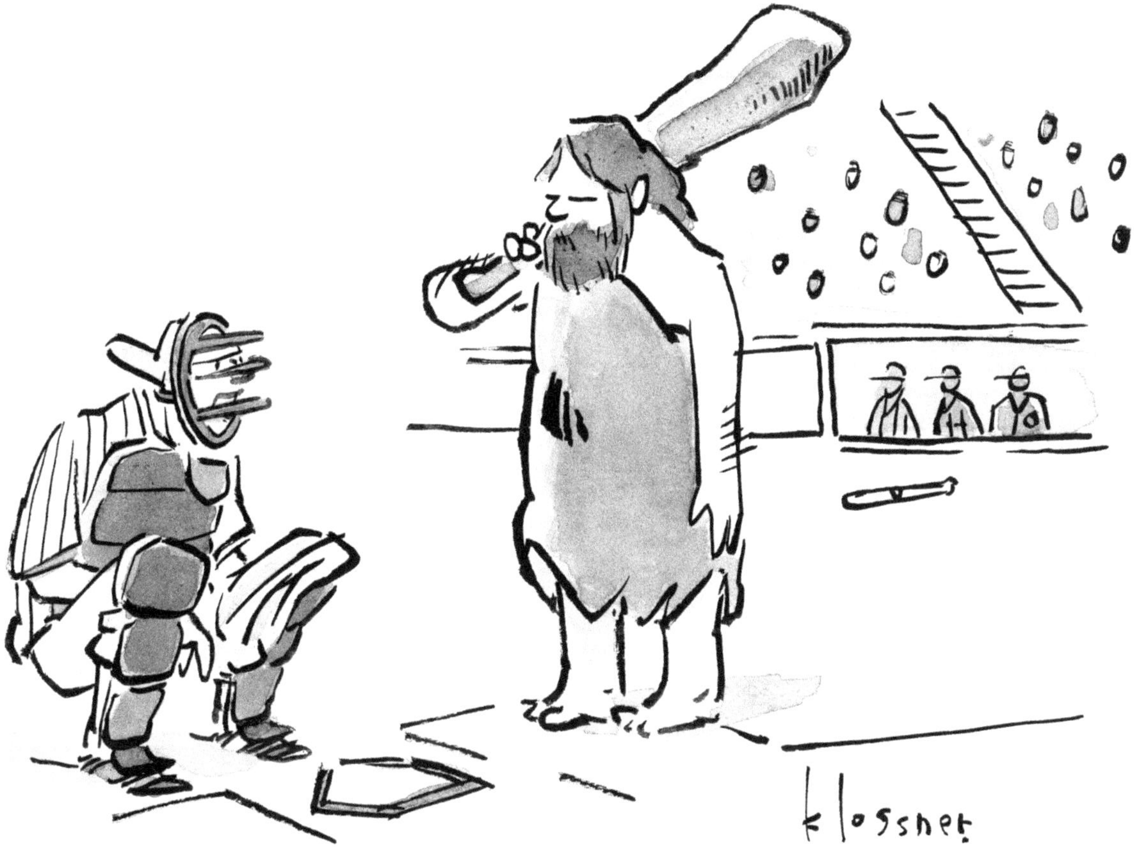
klossner

"A lot has happened since your last at-bat."

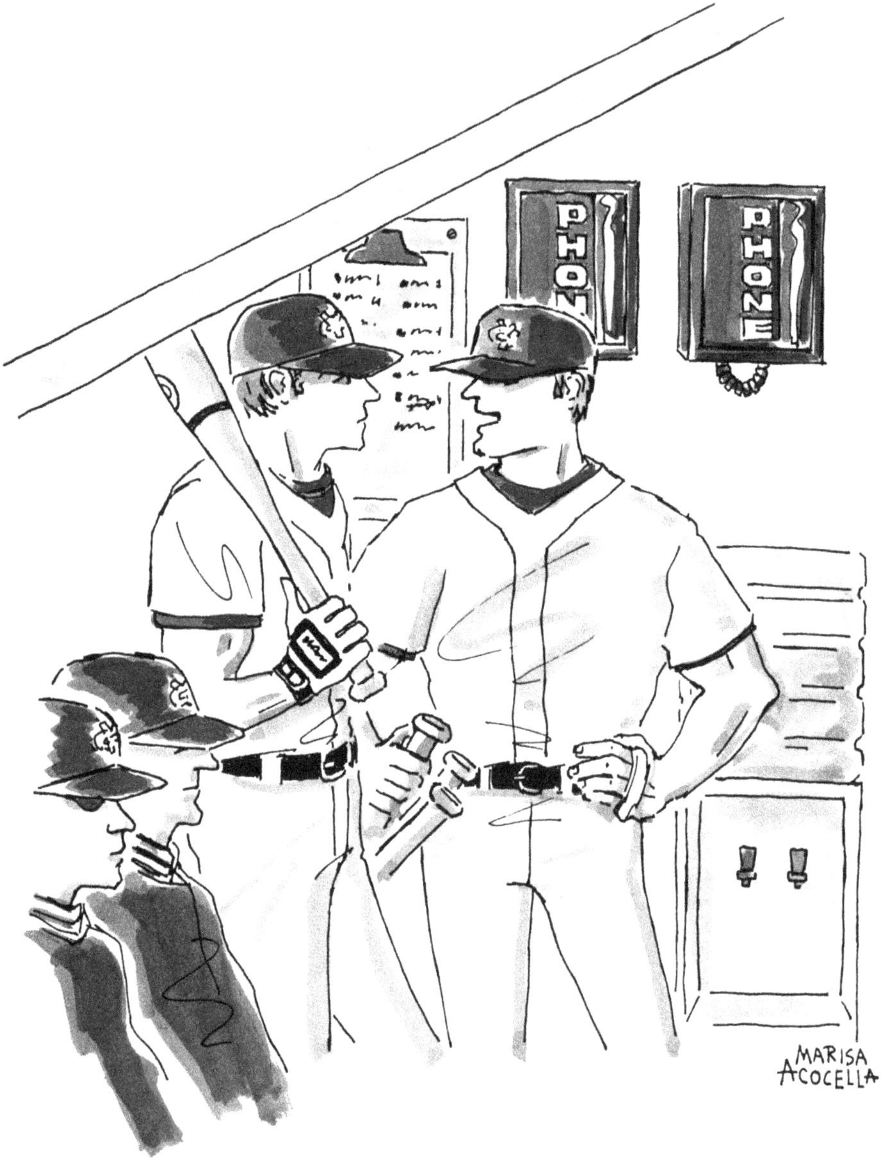
PHONE
PHONE
MARISA ACOCELLA

"Look, I'm the bobblehead of this team."

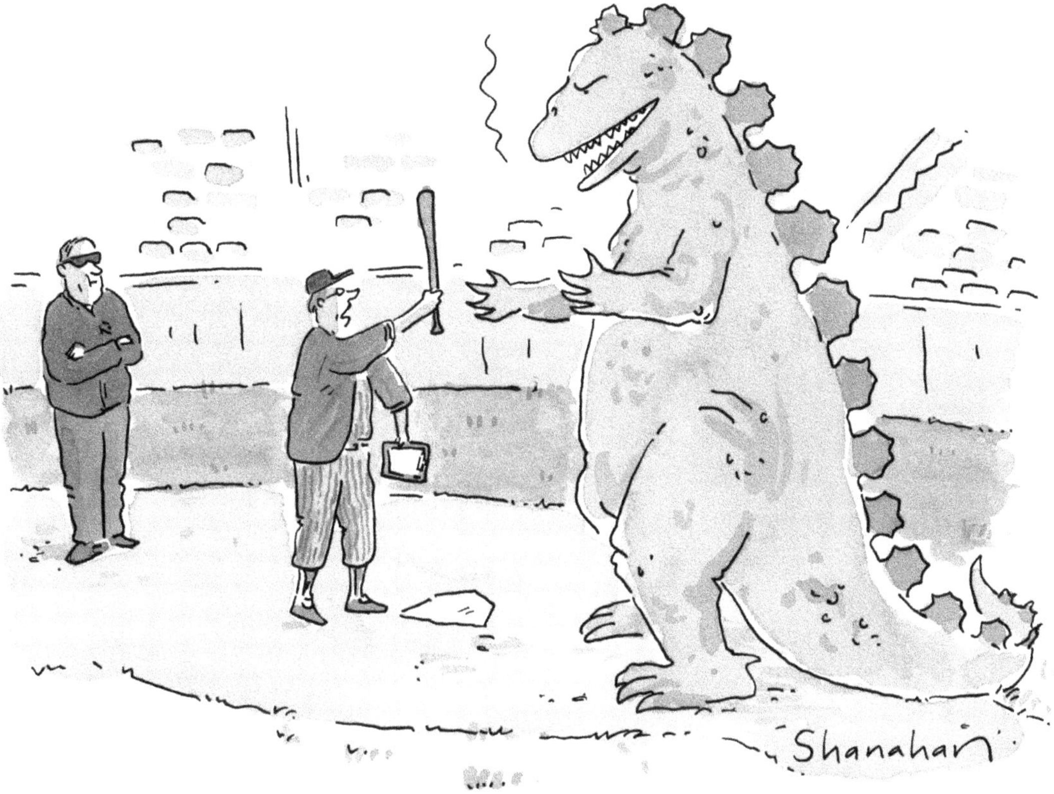
Shanahan

"Let's show Mr. Steinbrenner what you can do."

"I have very expressive eyes."

Shanahan

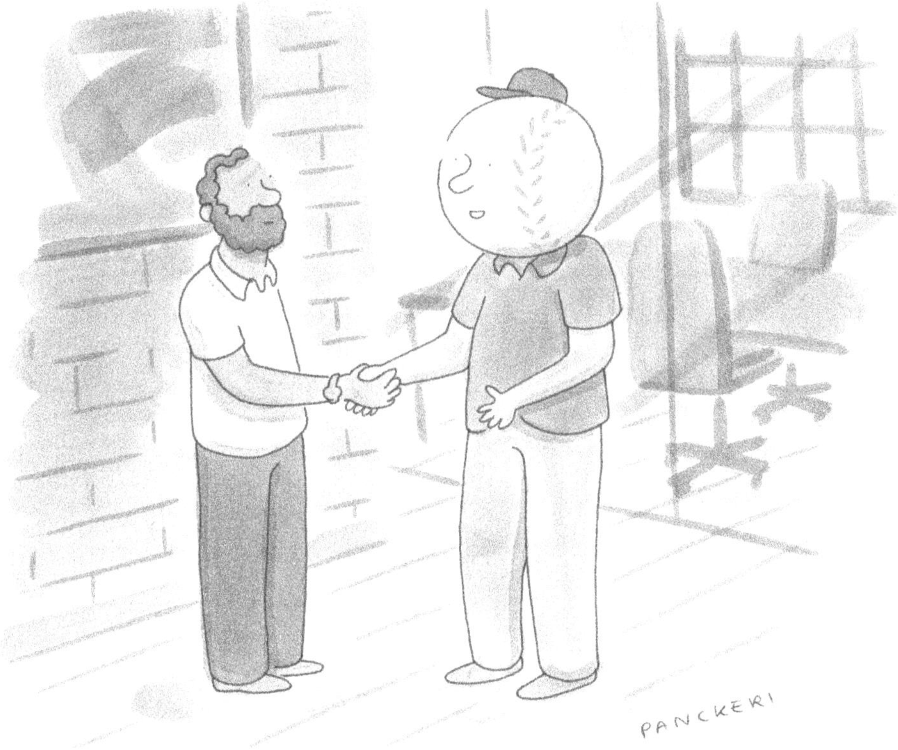
PANCKERI

"Please call me Michael—Mr. Met is my father's name."

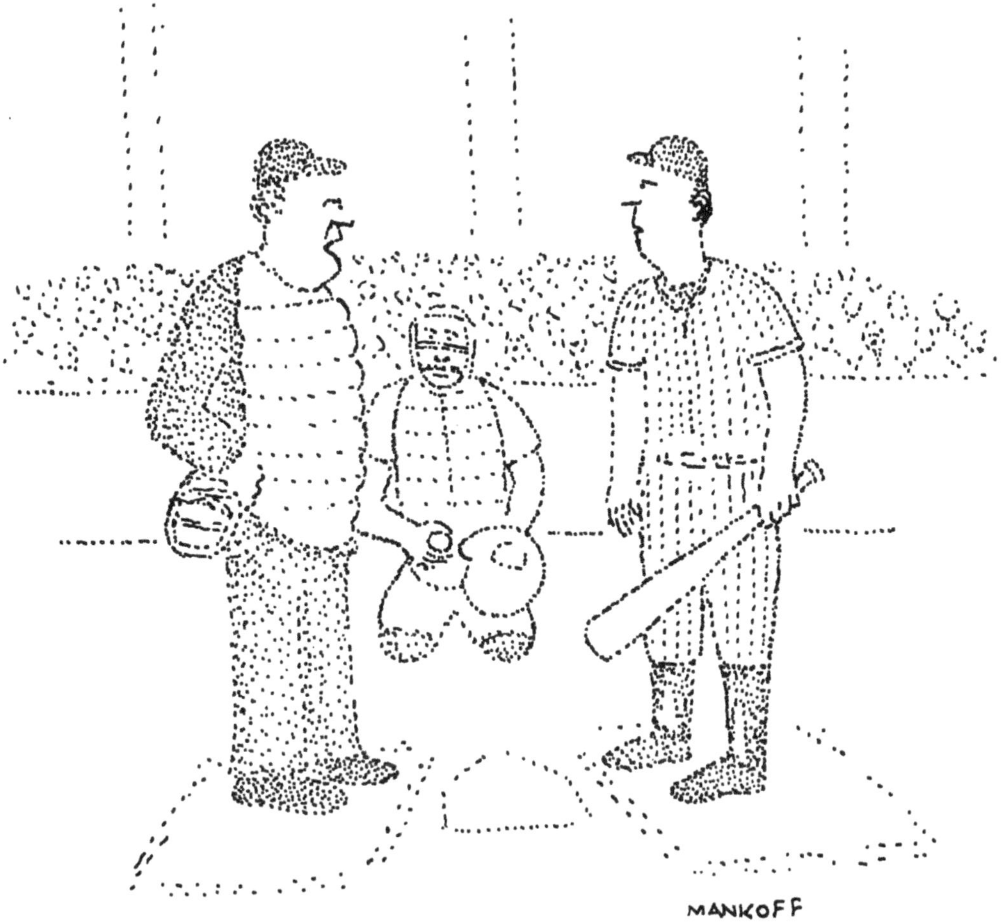
MANKOFF

"All right! Have it your own way. It was a ball."

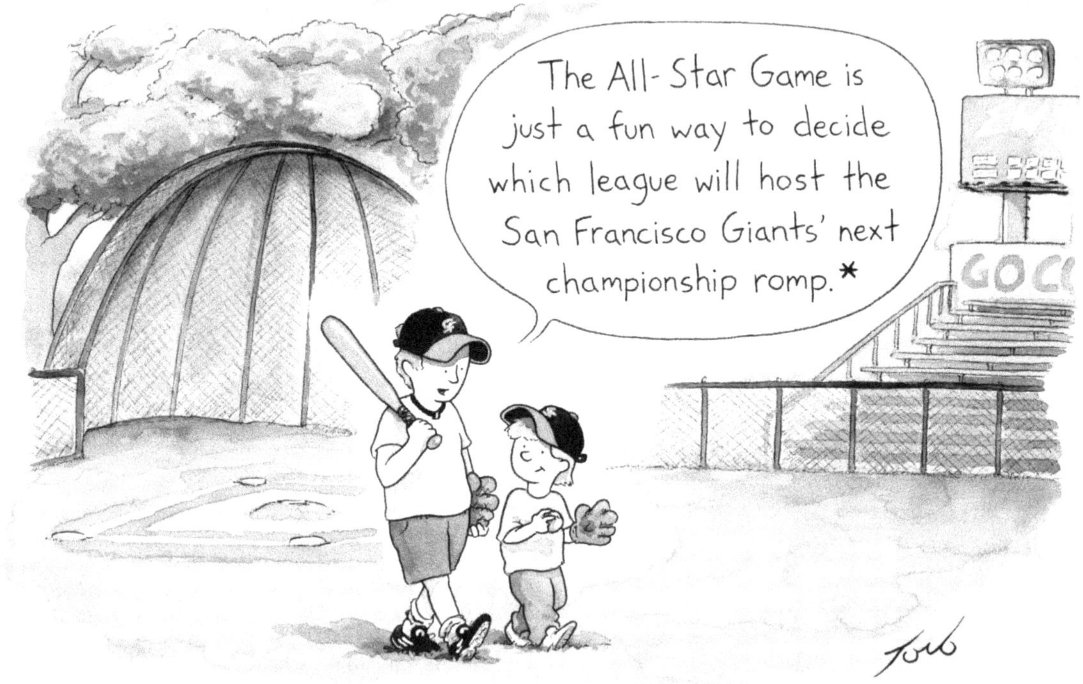
The All-Star Game is just a fun way to decide which league will host the San Francisco Giants' next championship romp.*

* The artist IN NO WAY apologizes for his flagrant bias

EDITOR'S NOTE: THE CARTOON DEPARTMENT DOES NOT CONDONE THE VIEWS AND OPINIONS EXPRESSED IN THIS PIECE, SINCE WE ARE TERRIBLY MISGUIDED YANKEES FANS

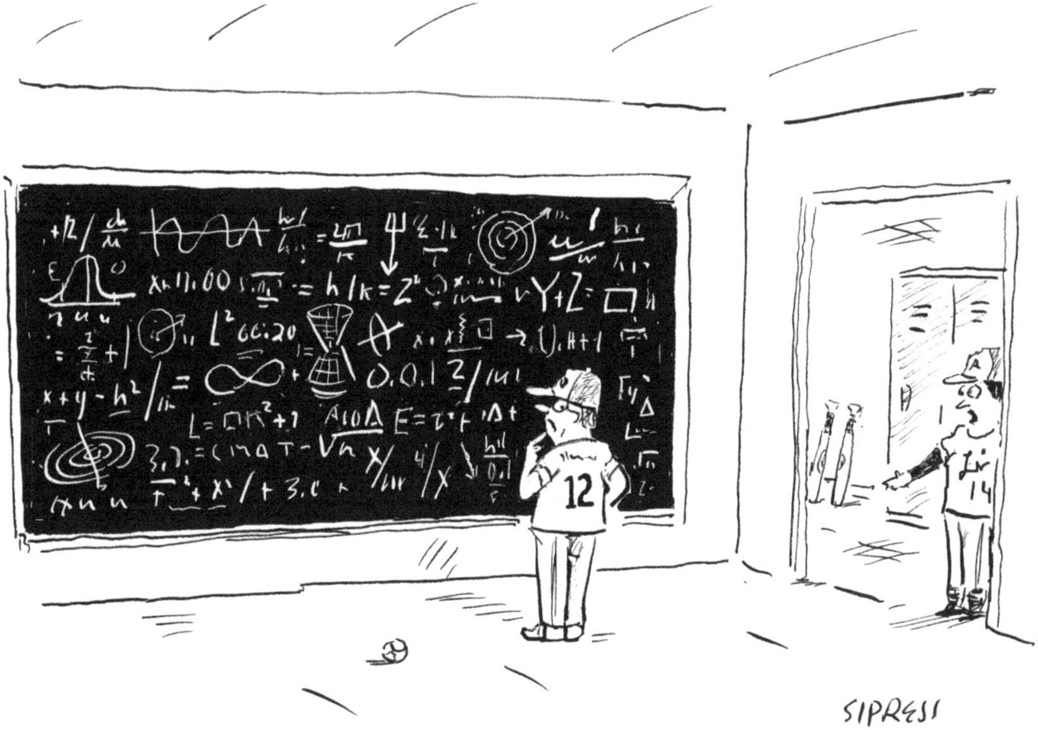
12
SIPRESI

"Figured out who should bat cleanup yet, Skipper?"

"Would you explain to your son that there's no free agency in T-ball?"

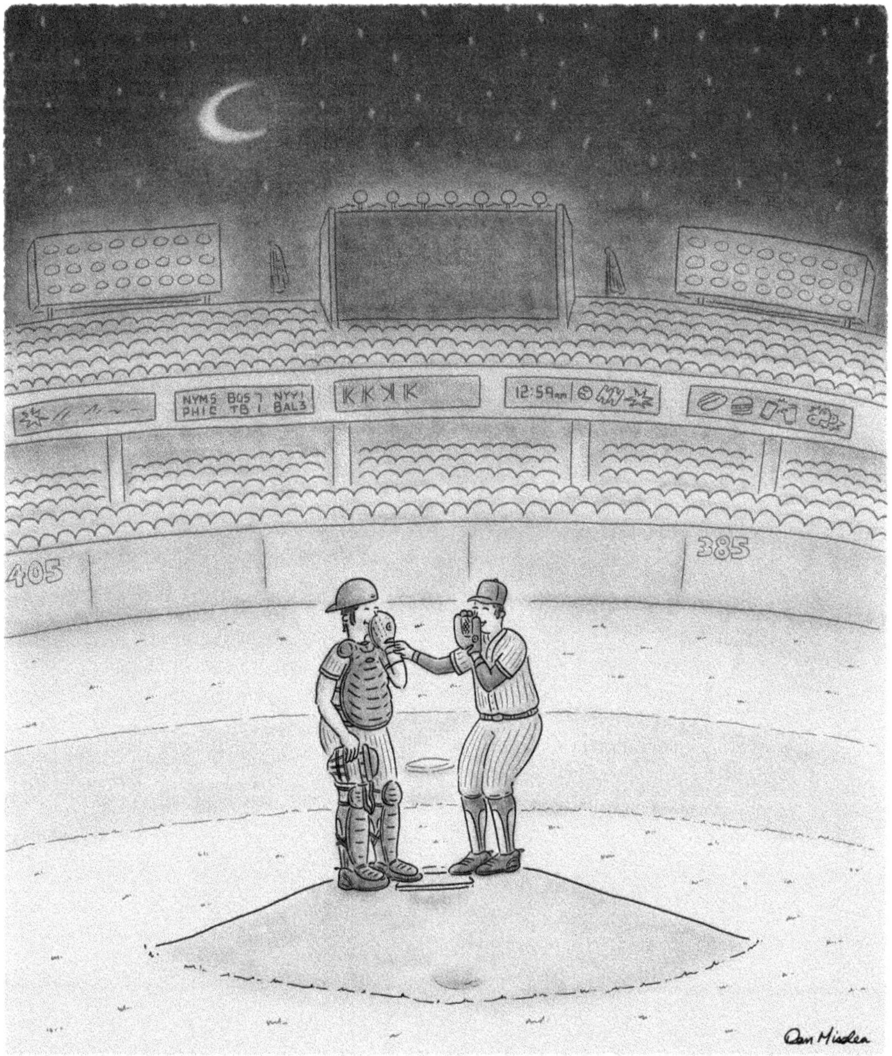
NYM 5 BOS 7 NYY 1
PHI 6 TB 1 BAL 3
KKKK
12:59am
405
385

"Oh, my God, have we been talking all night?"

"Then we're agreed—it's a great day for a ball game."

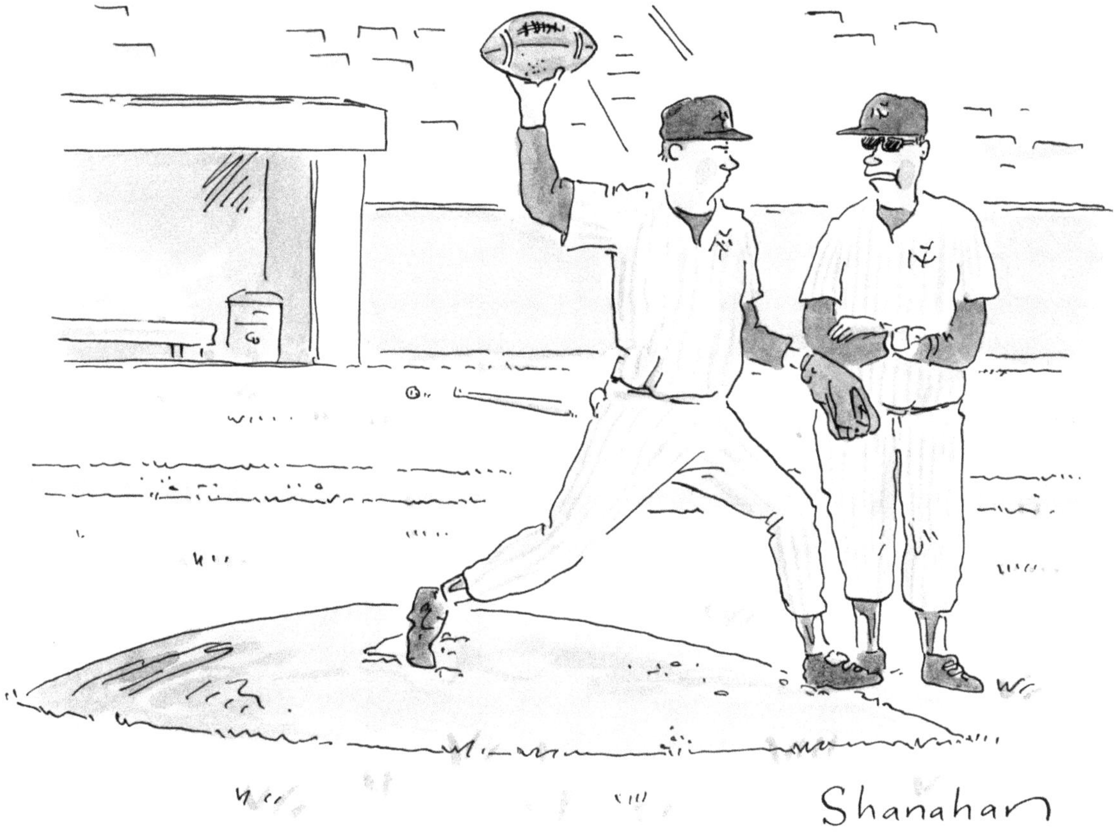
Shanahan

"There's your problem."

CBarsotti

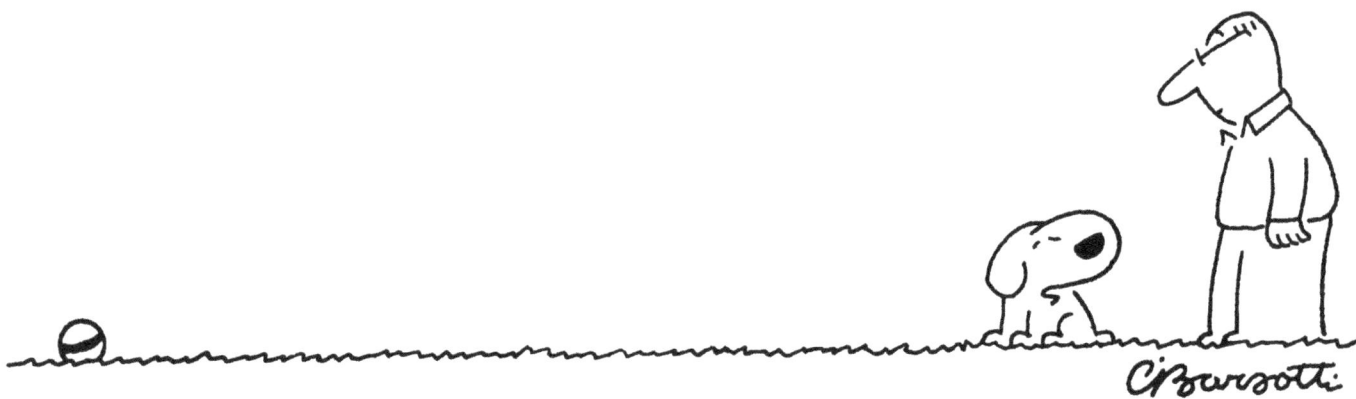

"Good arm."

"Let's go slider, fastball, curve, beanball, fight, ejection, shower, beer."

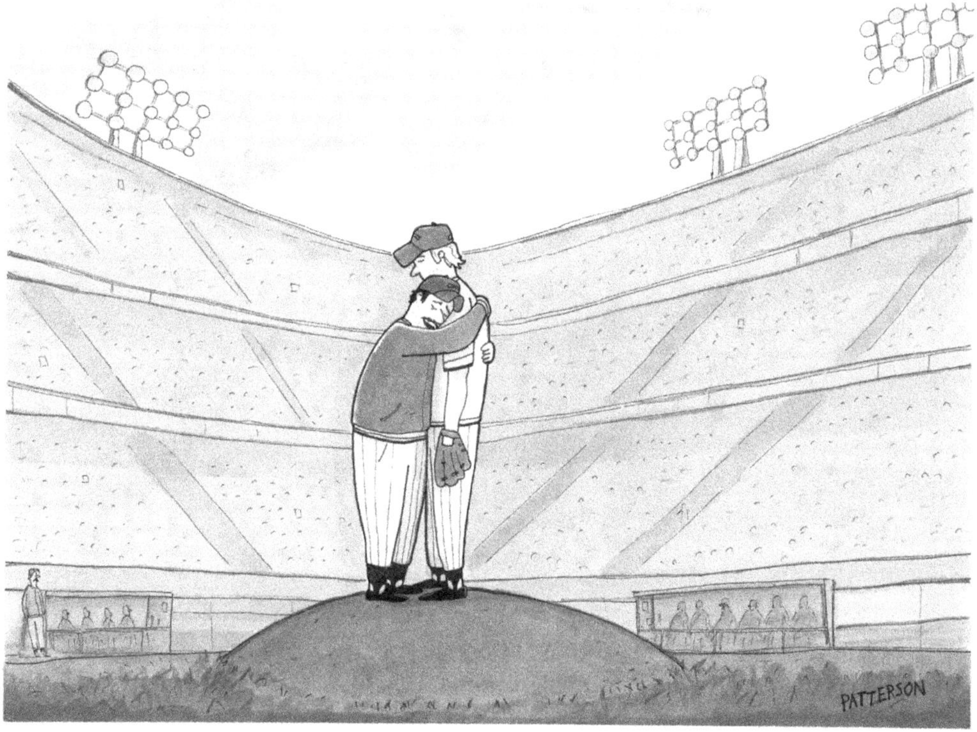
PATTERSON

"I love you. We all love you. Now throw some strikes."

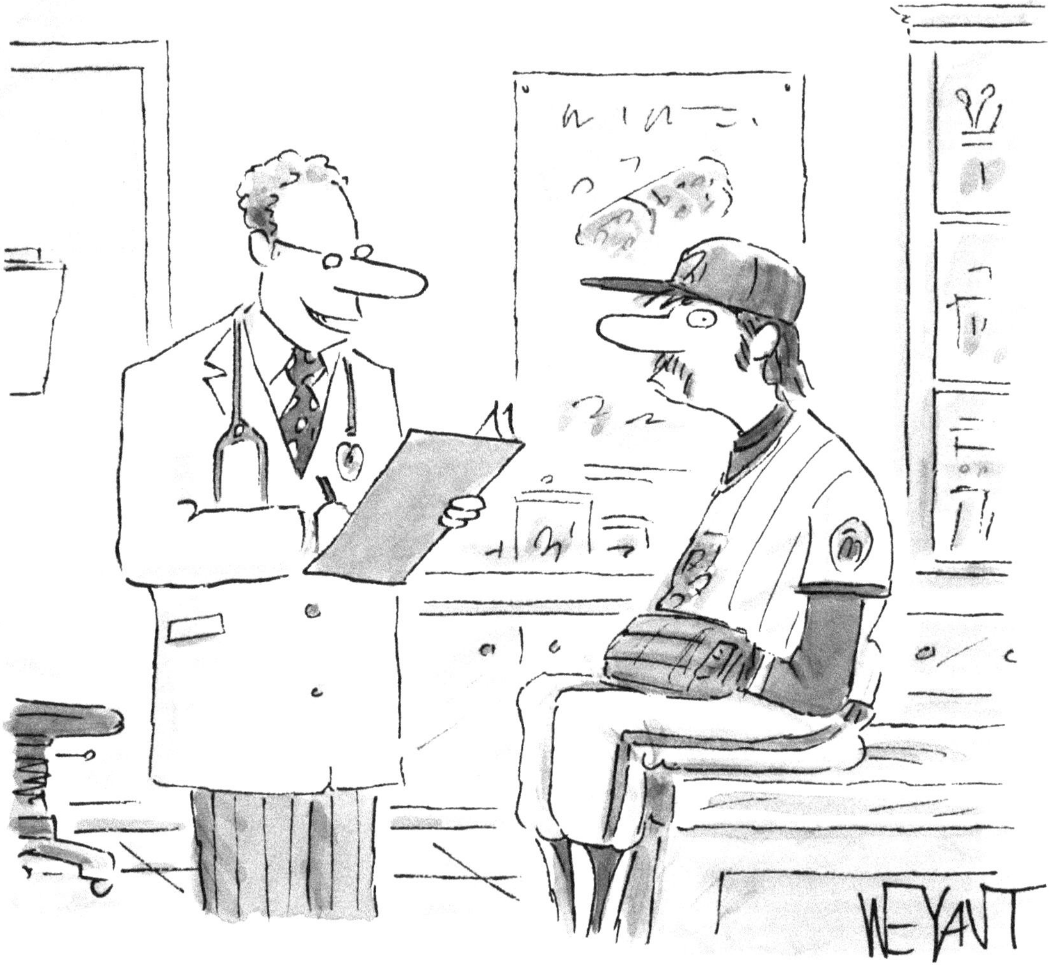
WEYANT

"The good news is it's the size of a baseball."

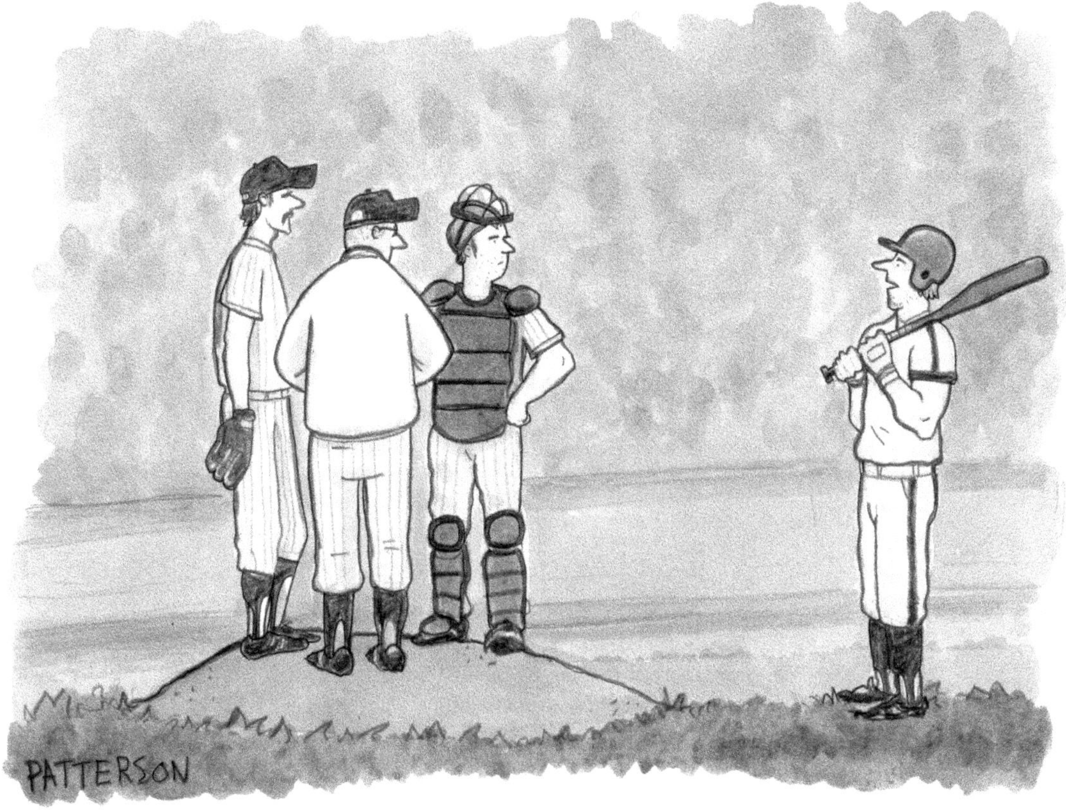
PATTERSON

"Want to know what I think?"

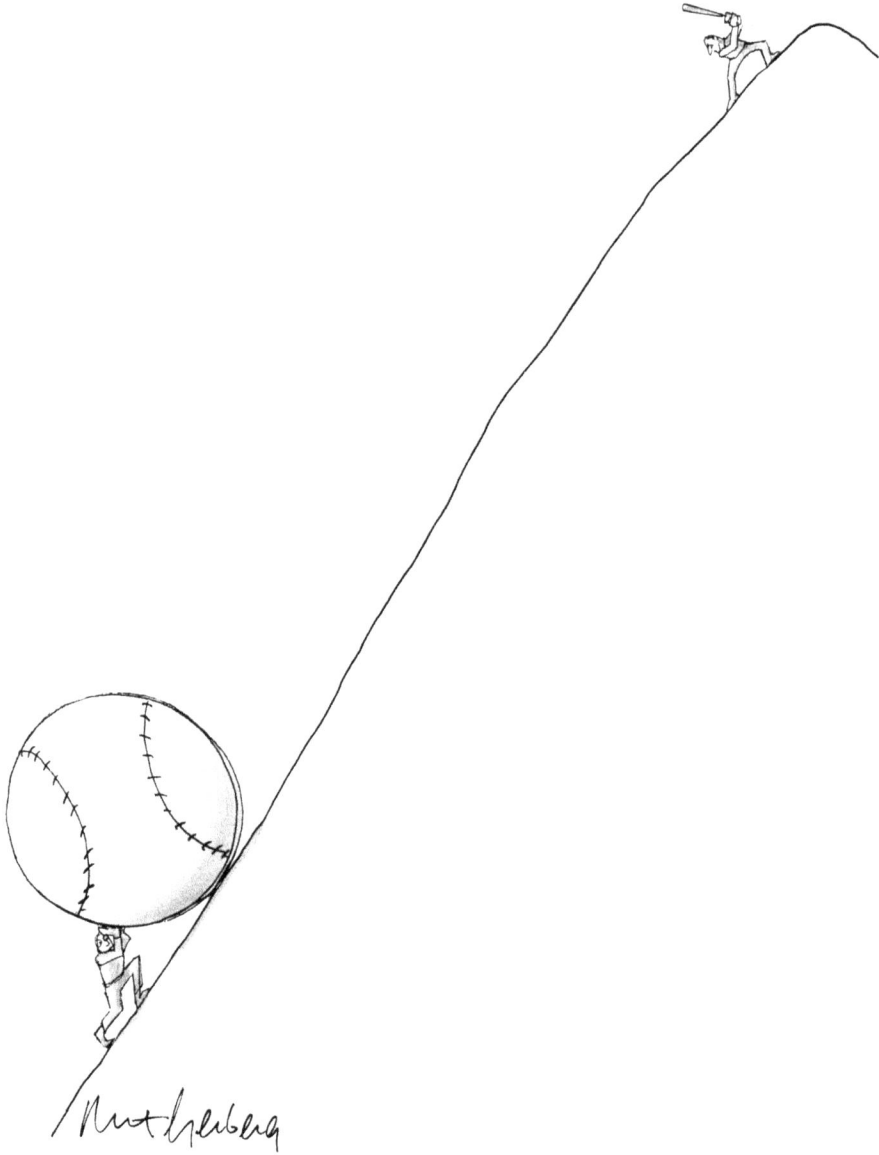

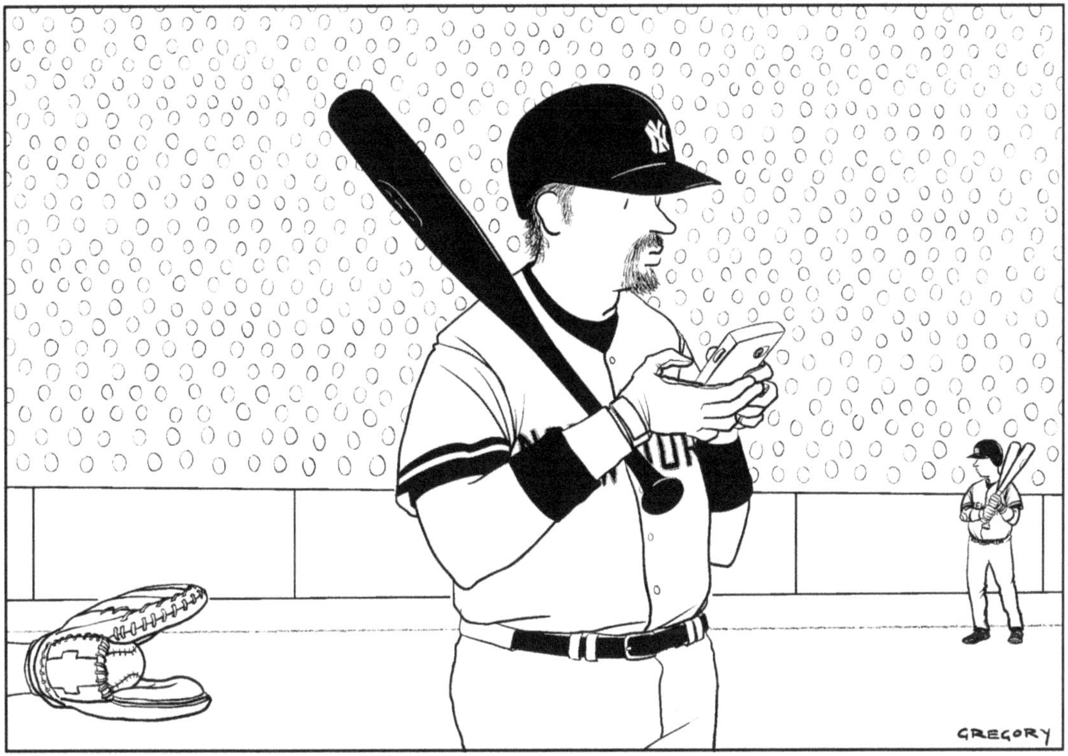
GREGORY

"hey fans! im at bat,. btm 9th, bases loaded, score tied--oops, jst got called strike1!"

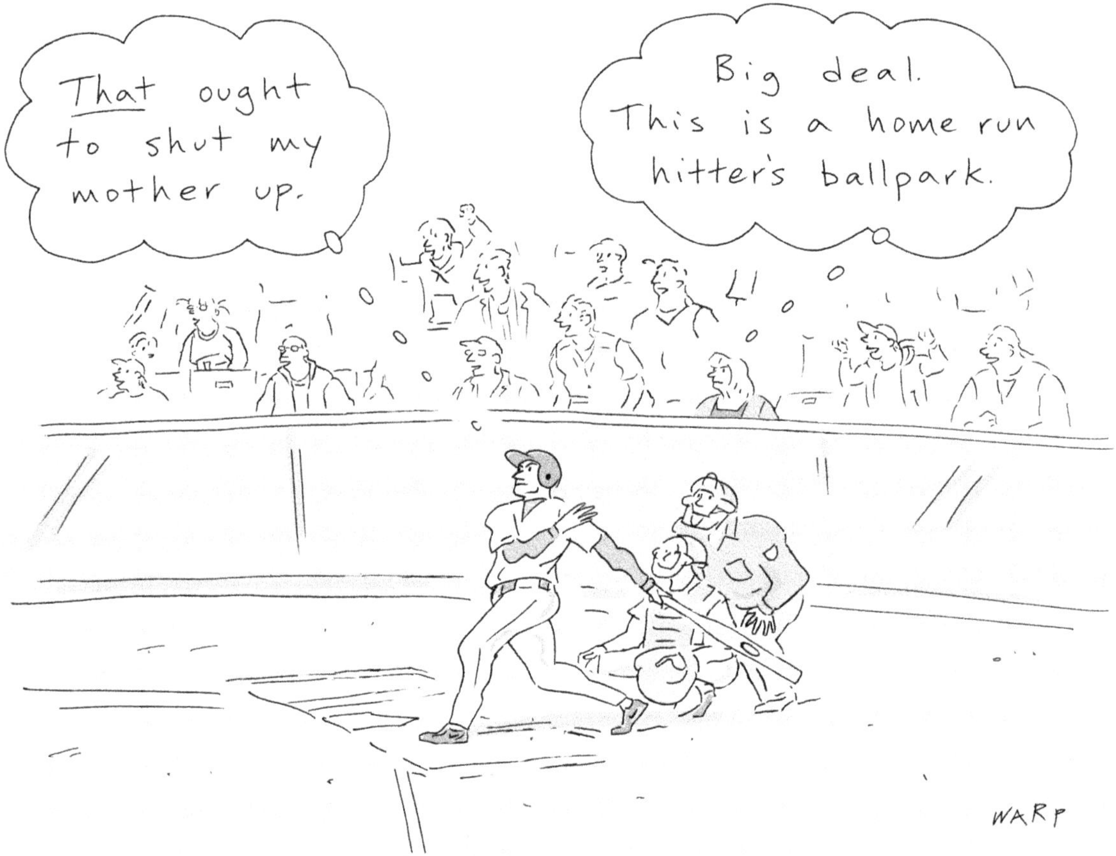
That ought to shut my mother up.
Big deal. This is a home run hitter's ballpark.
WARP

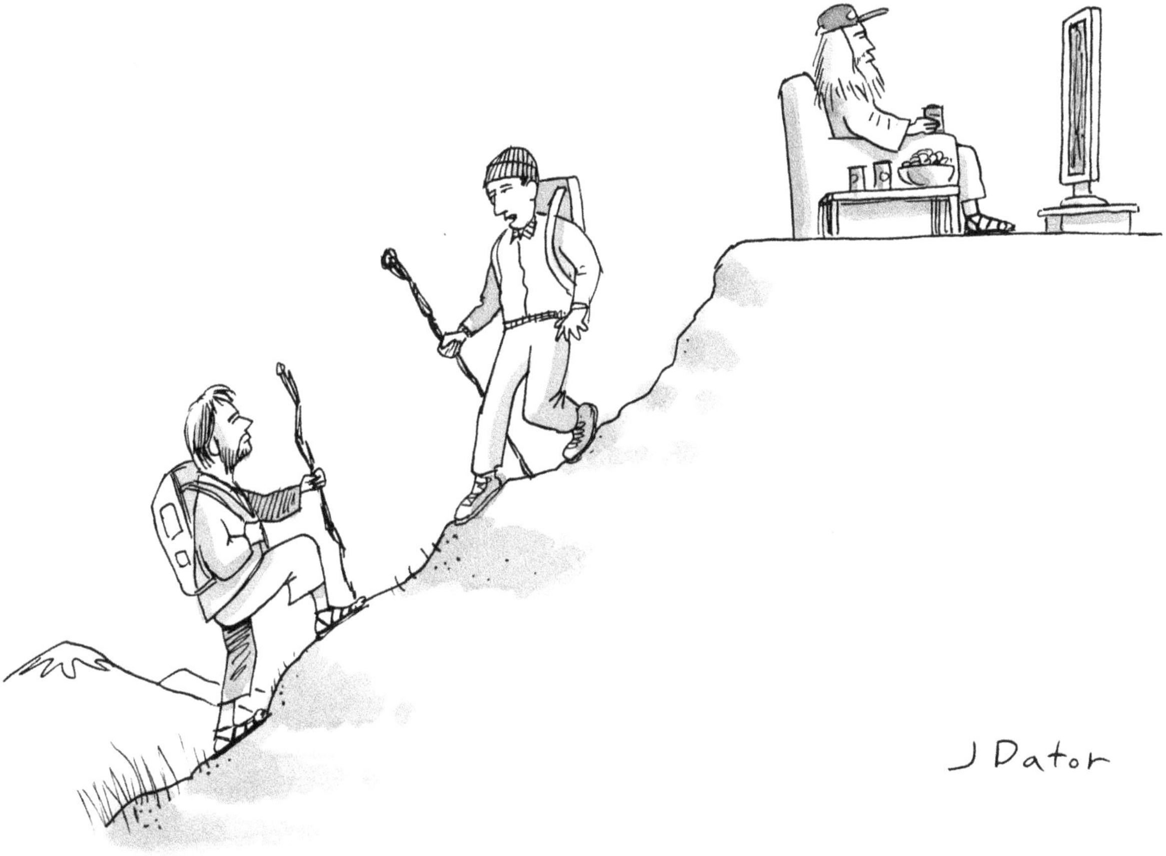
J Dator

"I hope you like sports metaphors."

"We've been standing here talking about how to pitch to
the batter for way too long, haven't we?"

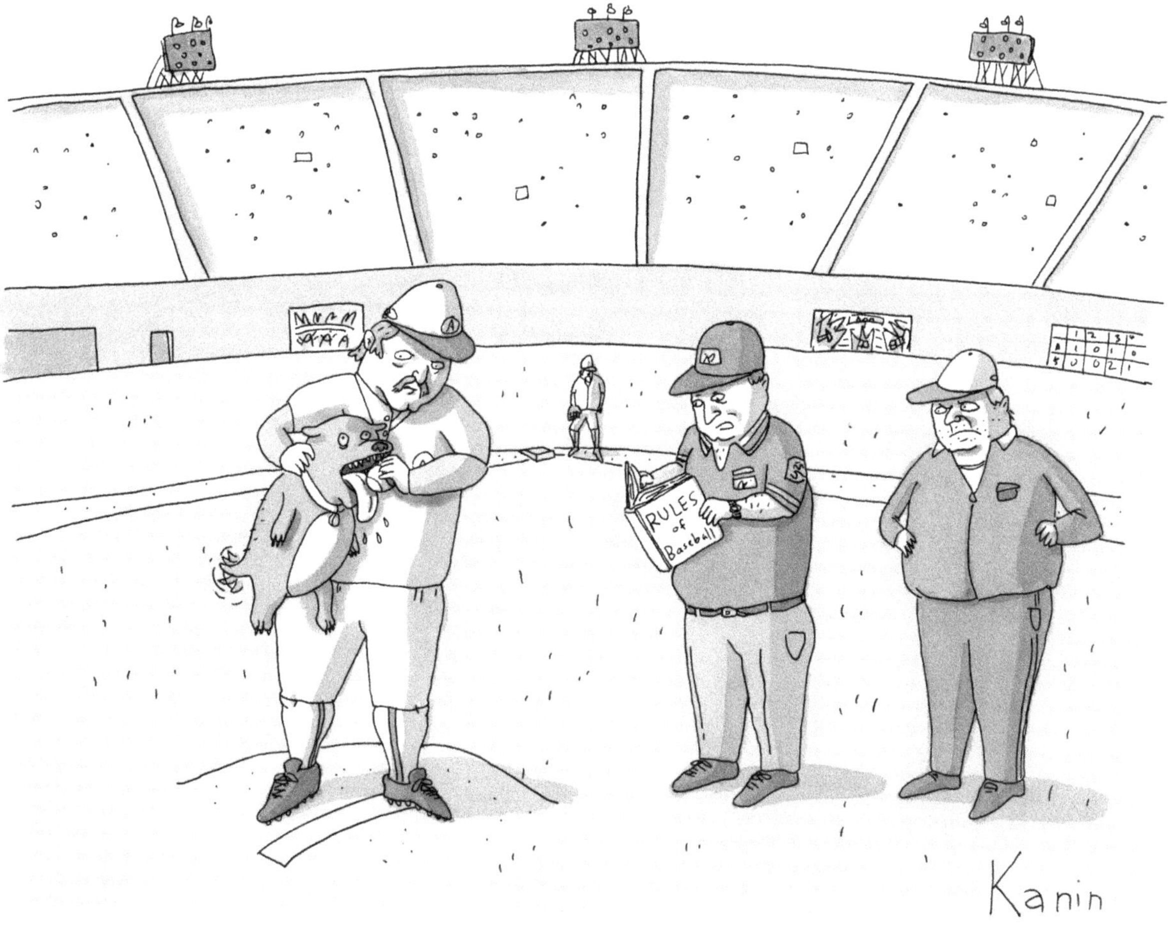
RULES of Baseball
Kanin

"I'm afraid he's right—there's nothing in here about slobber balls."

"Your inability to turn off your critical voice, combined with your fear of disappointing your overbearing, demanding father, is causing you to lose faith in your fastball."

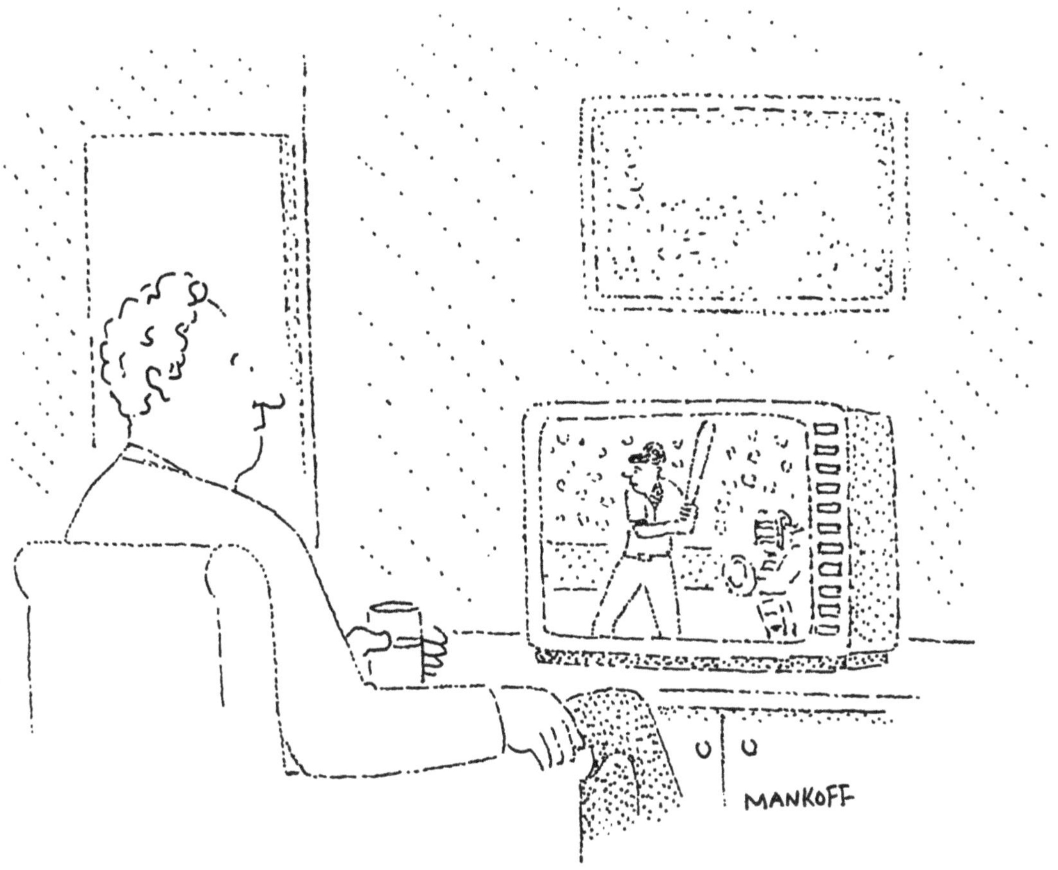
MANKOFF

"Ken bats left-handed, enjoys cultural as well as outdoor activities, and seeks a sensitive non-smoking woman for a lasting partnership that includes long walks, good music, and fielding practice."

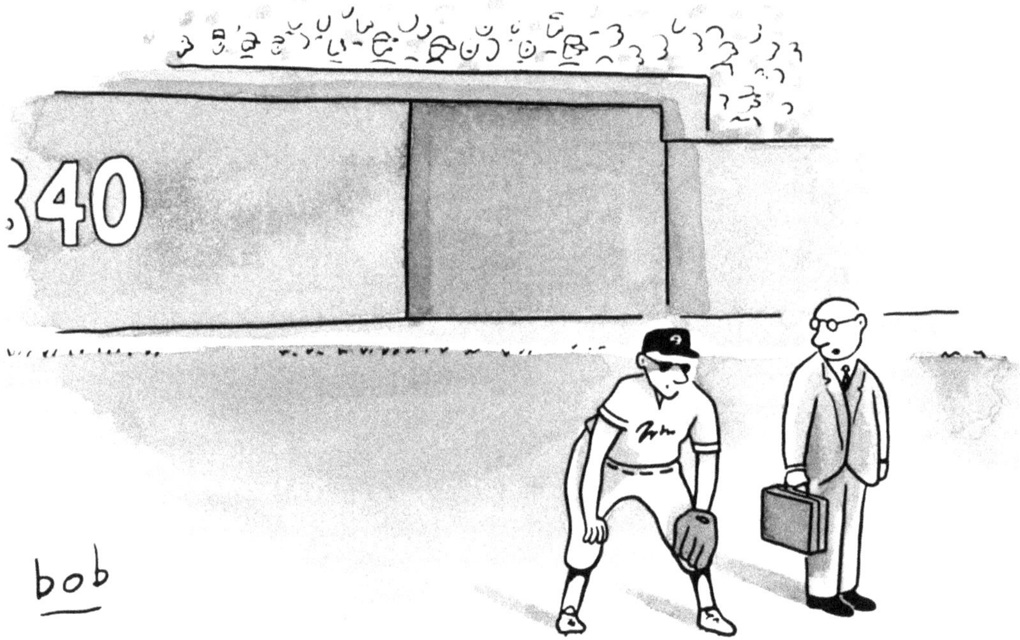
340
bob

"Just remember, if you give a hundred and ten per cent, I get twenty per cent of that."

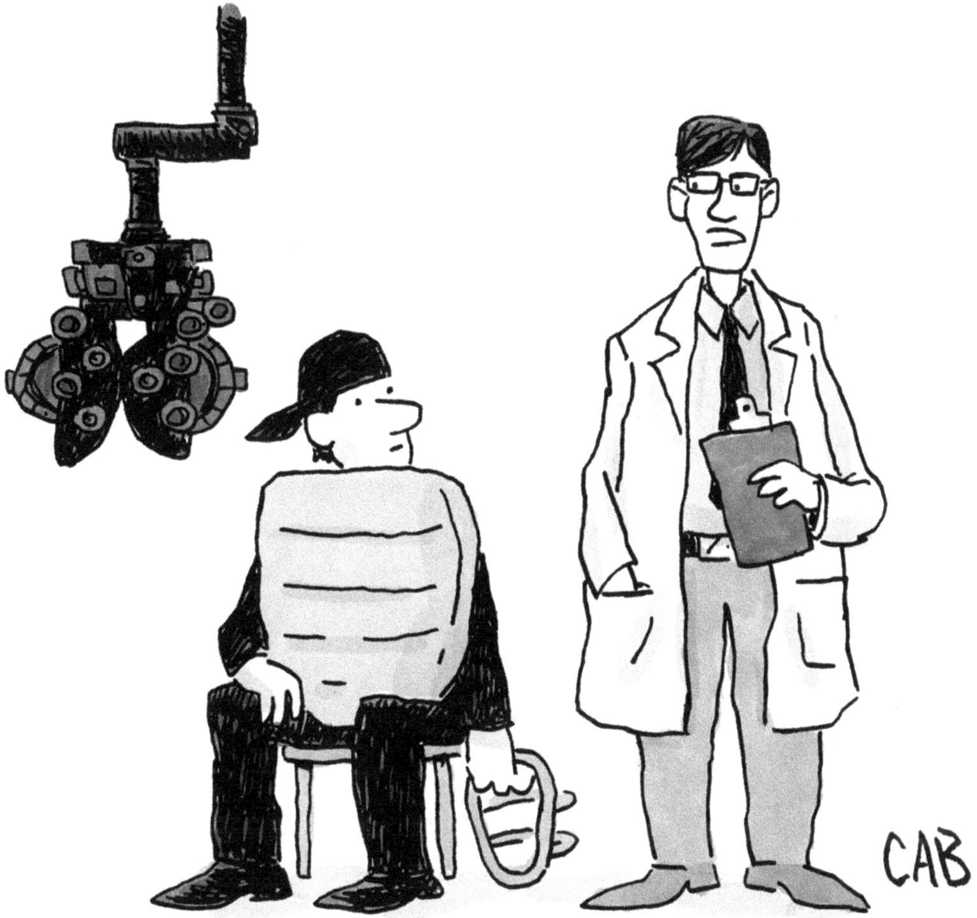
CAB

"They're right, you do need glasses."

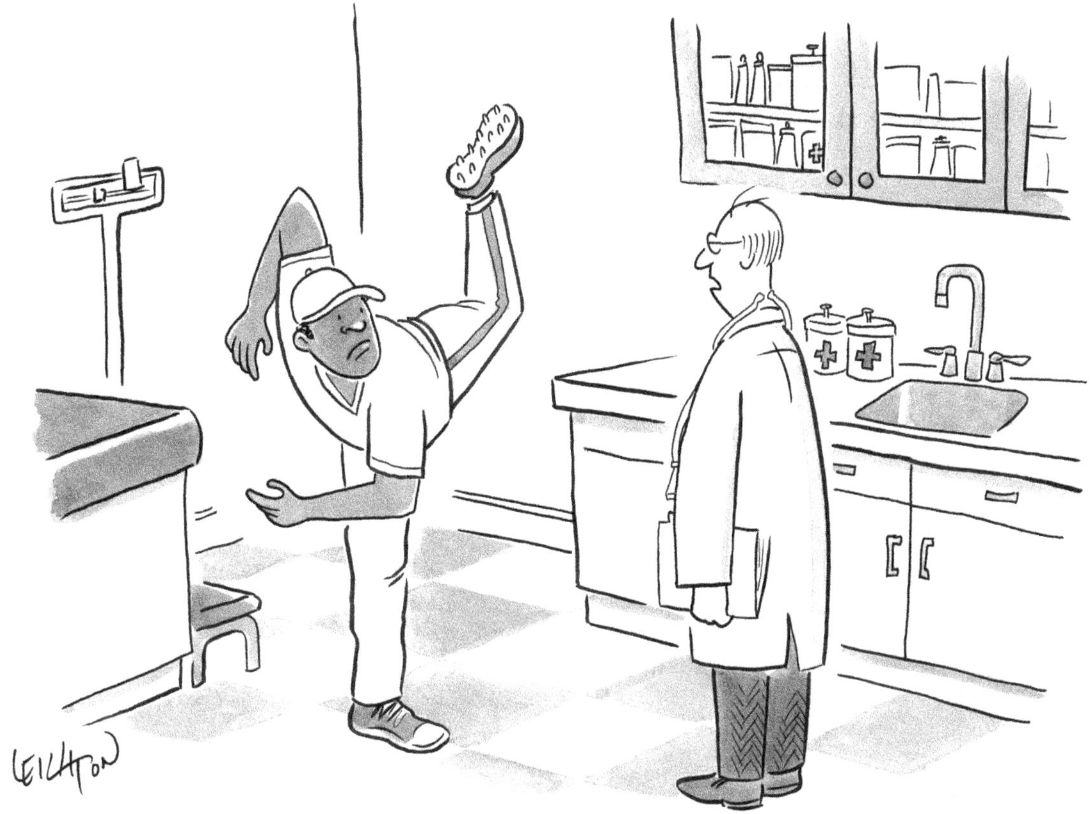
LEIGHTON

"Then don't do that."

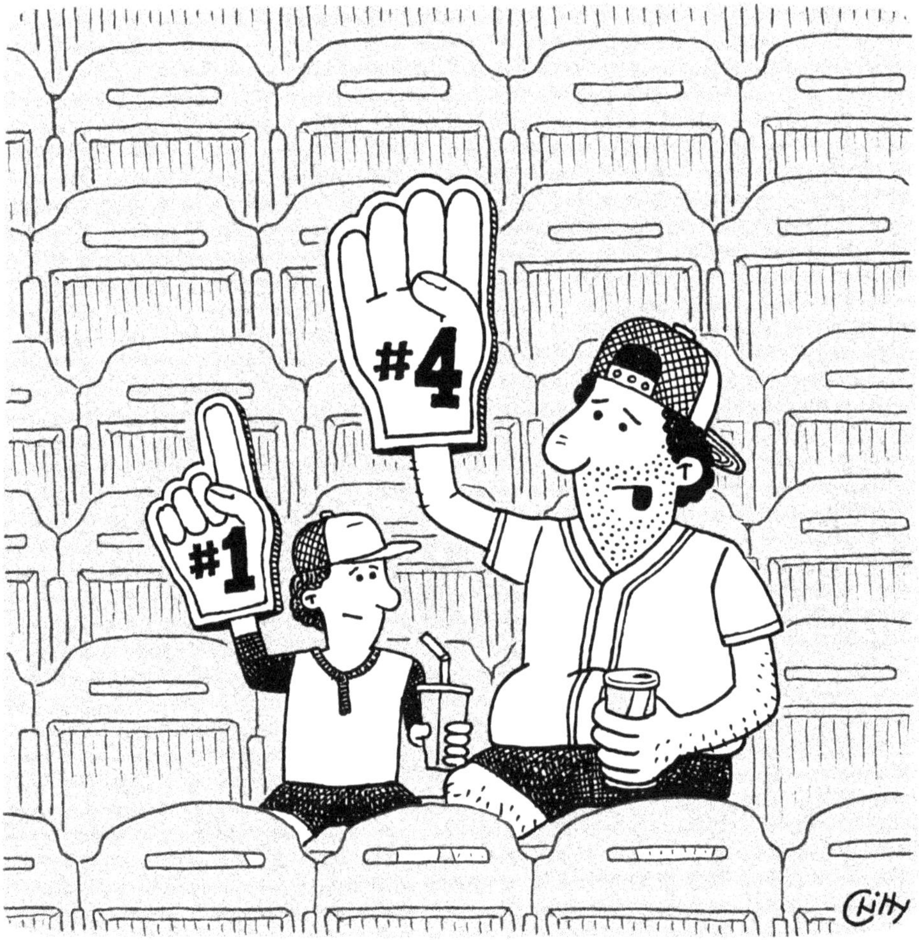
#4
#1
Chitty

"Ah, the innocence of youth. Enjoy it while it lasts."

"My husband wants to know if the sonogram
can tell if the baby is a Red Sox or Yankees fan."

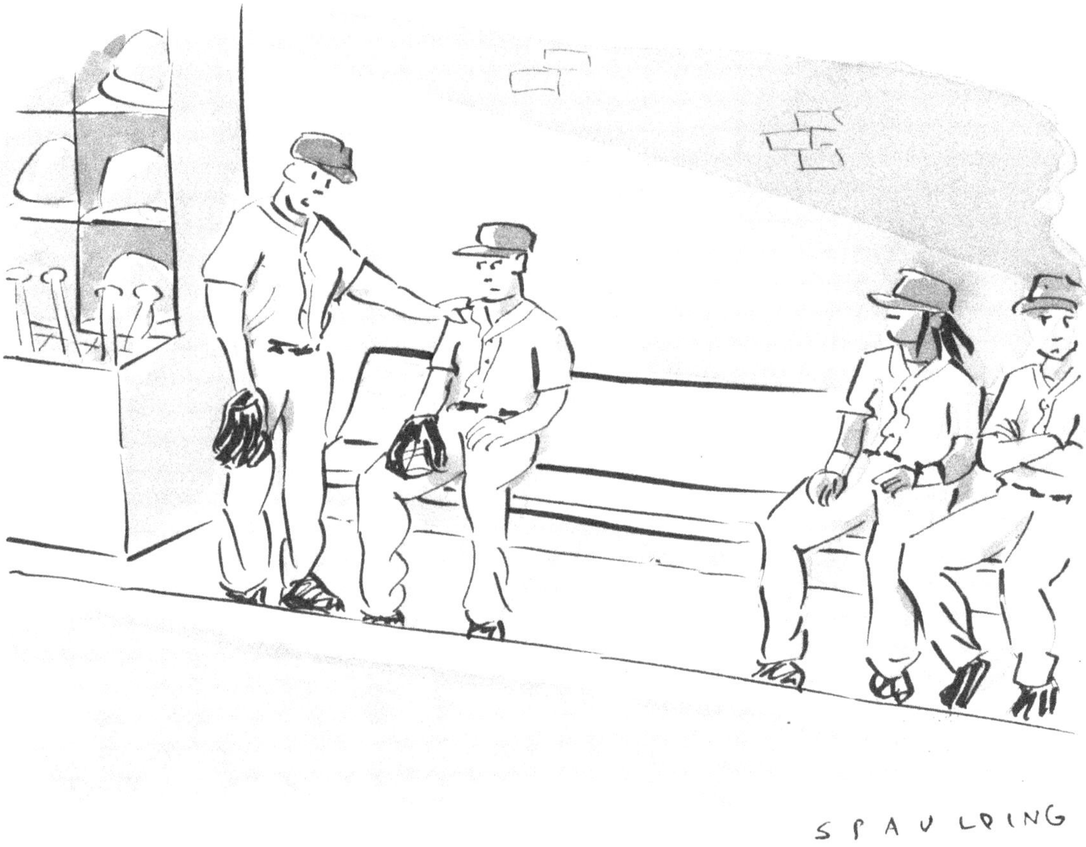
SPAULDING

"Hey—if you ever want to talk about this no hitter, I'm here."

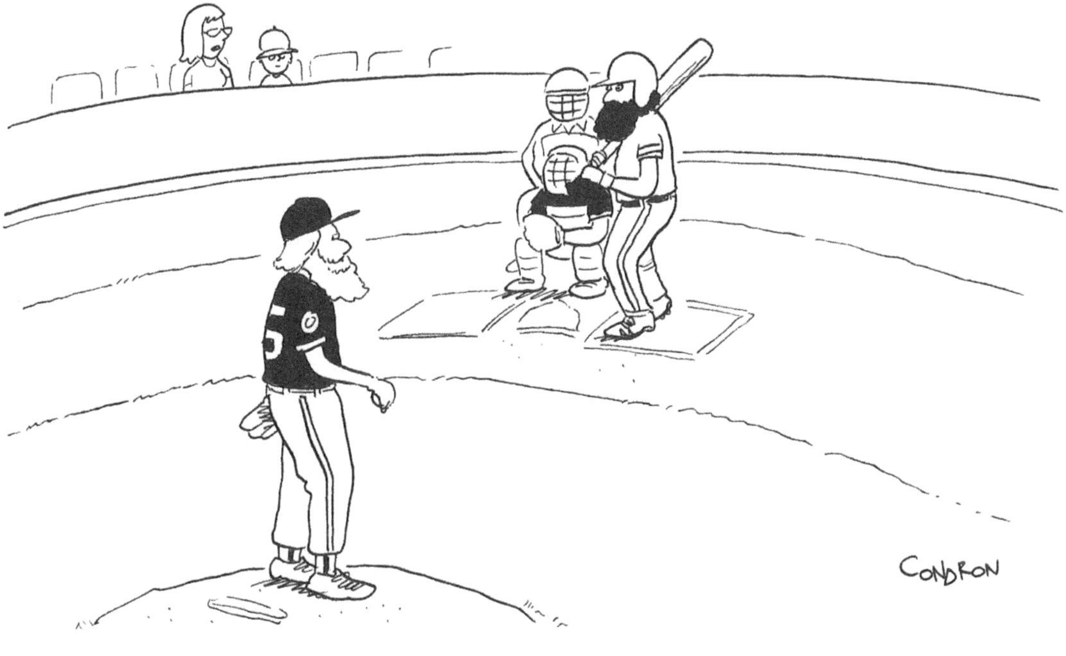
CONDRON

"Hard to believe they both started this at bat clean-shaven."

"Deep Right Field: A Memoir..."

"Davis, grab a bat. You're hitting for Kelly.
I just can't listen to his walk-up song one more time."

"Charlie, it's us, your teammates. We're here to help you. The other team's getting an awful lot of hits and we're worried."

"'An easy fly ball to center field' – We'll see about that."

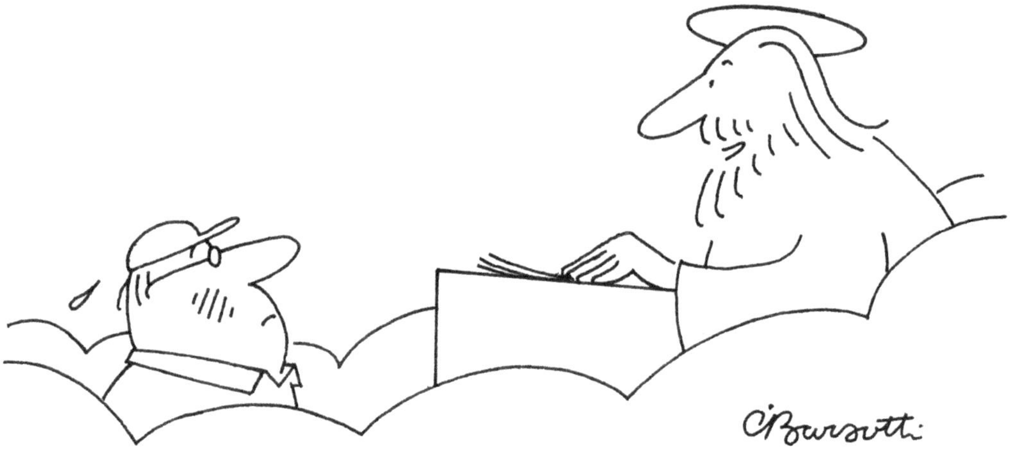
CBarsotti

"But you held on to that fly ball."

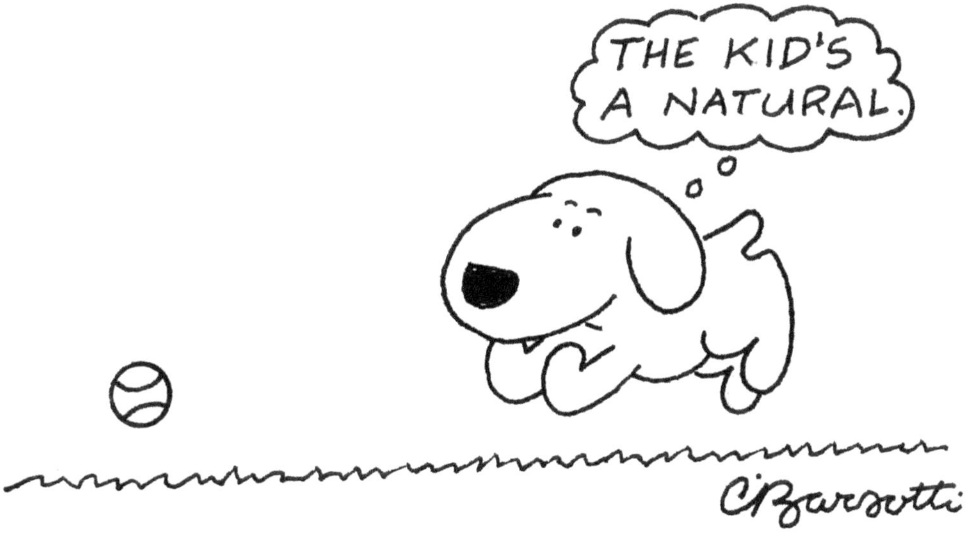
THE KID'S A NATURAL.
CBarsotti

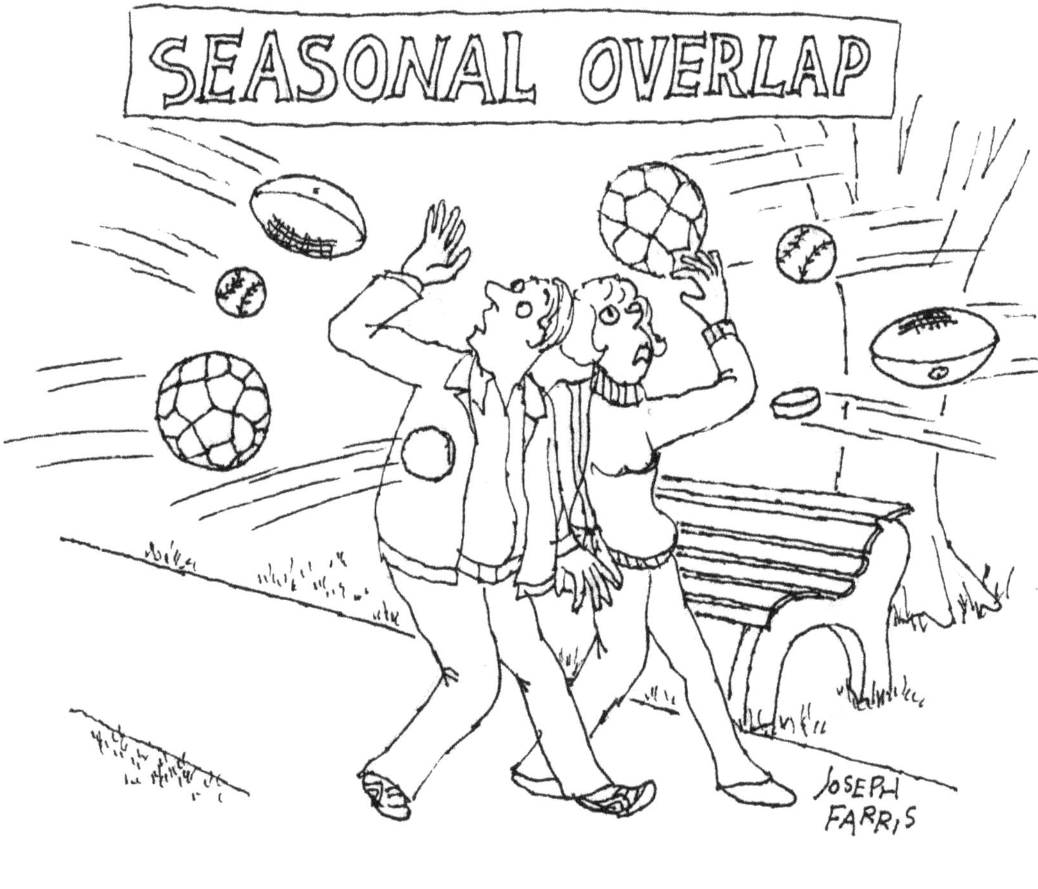
SEASONAL OVERLAP
JOSEPH FARRIS

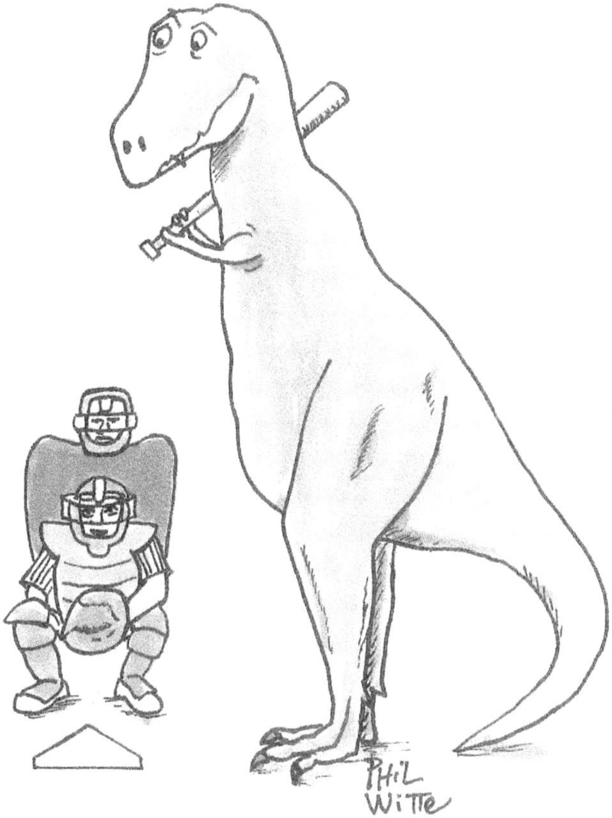
PHIL
WITTE

"Easy out, easy out."

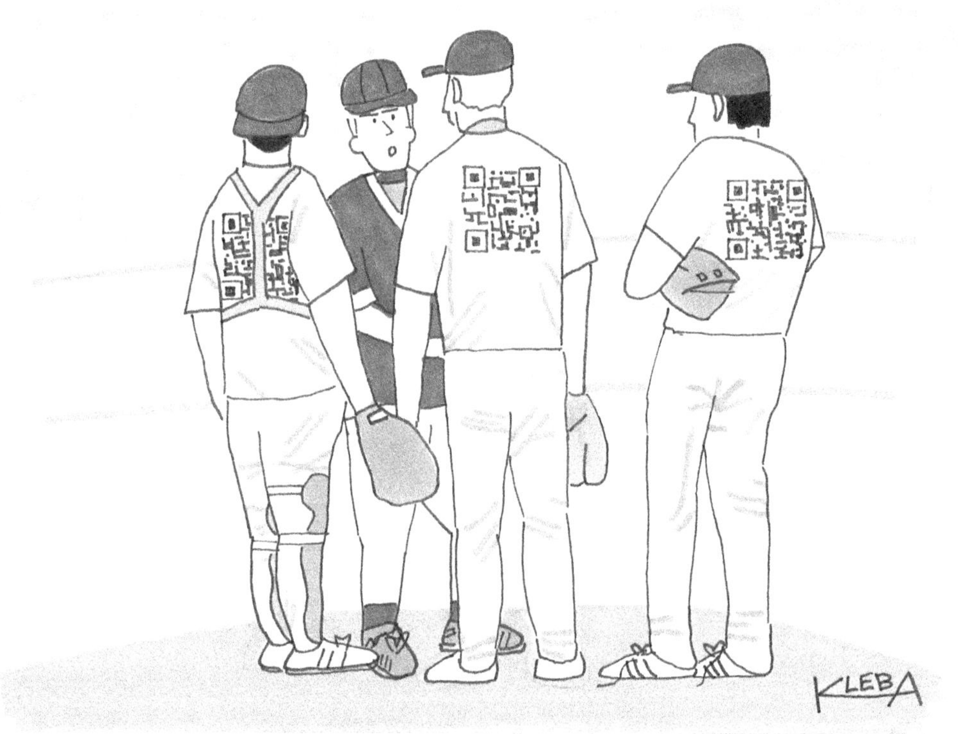
KLEBA

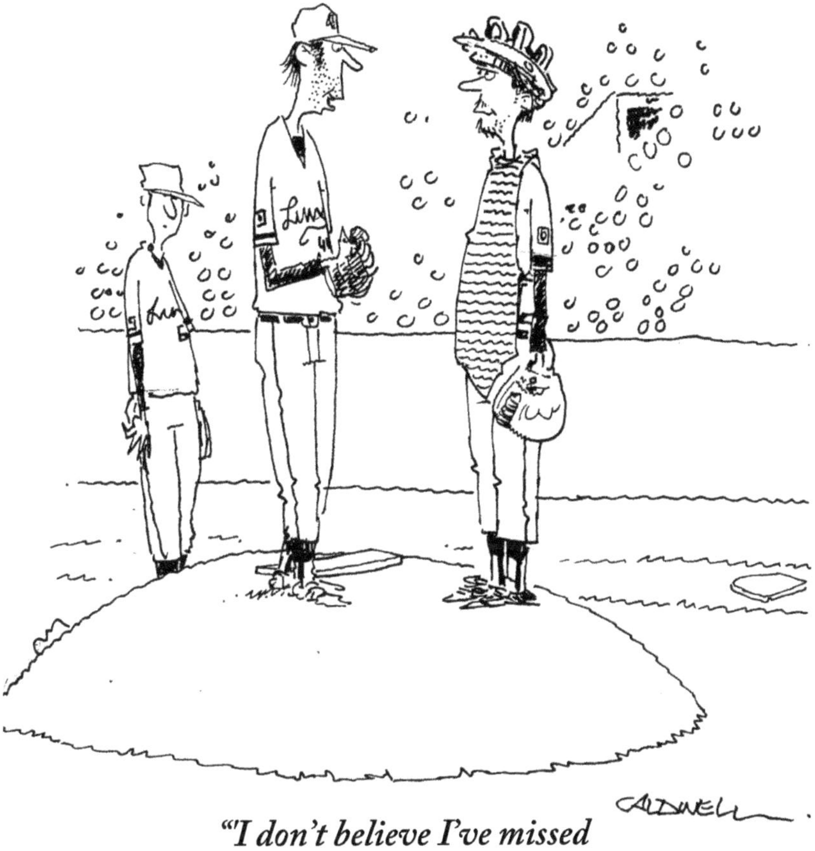
CALDWELL

"I don't believe I've missed a single sign since you made the switch to Power Point."

THE END OF THE BASEBALL SEASON IS NEAR

PHiL WiTTe

Play Ball!

Lander
McConnell

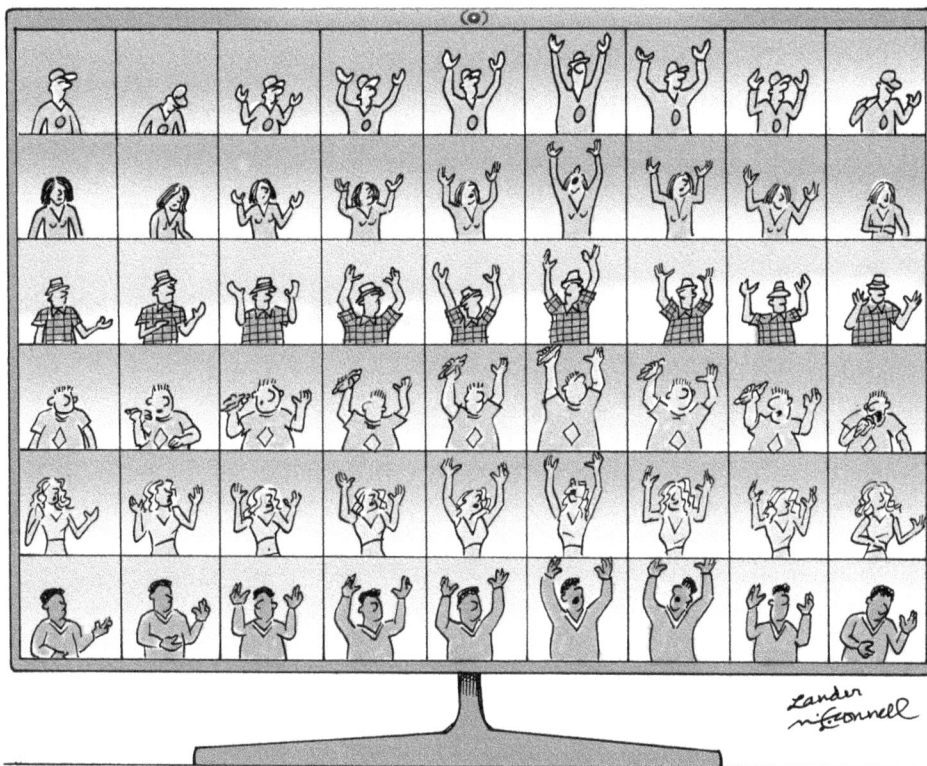

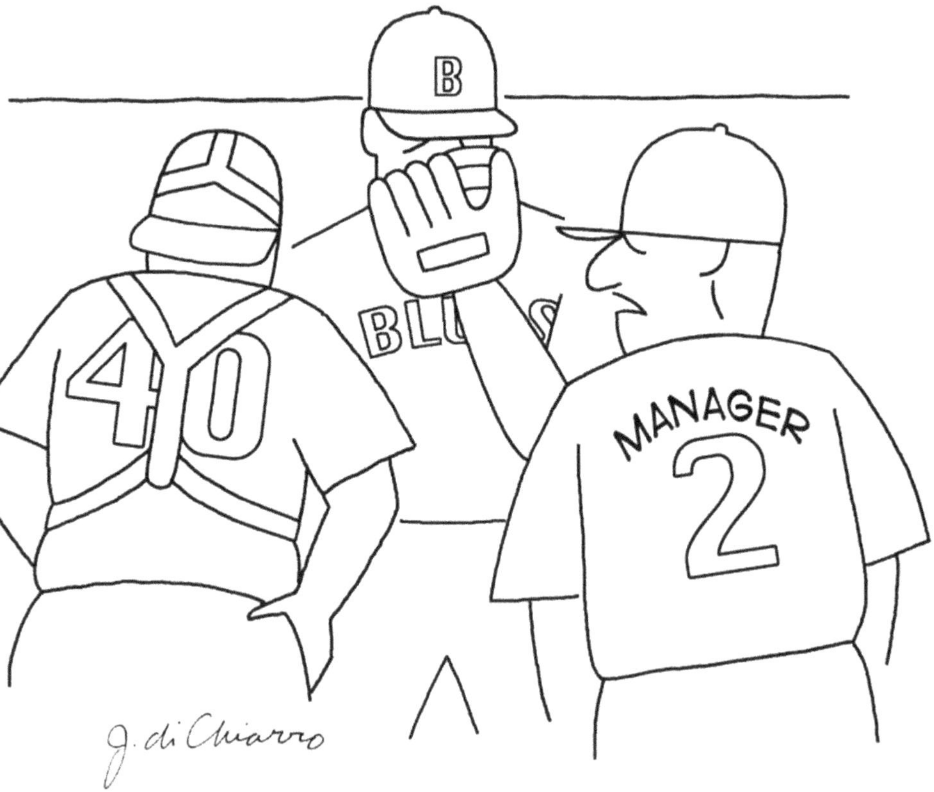
B
BLU
40
MANAGER
2

"We can't understand a word you're saying."

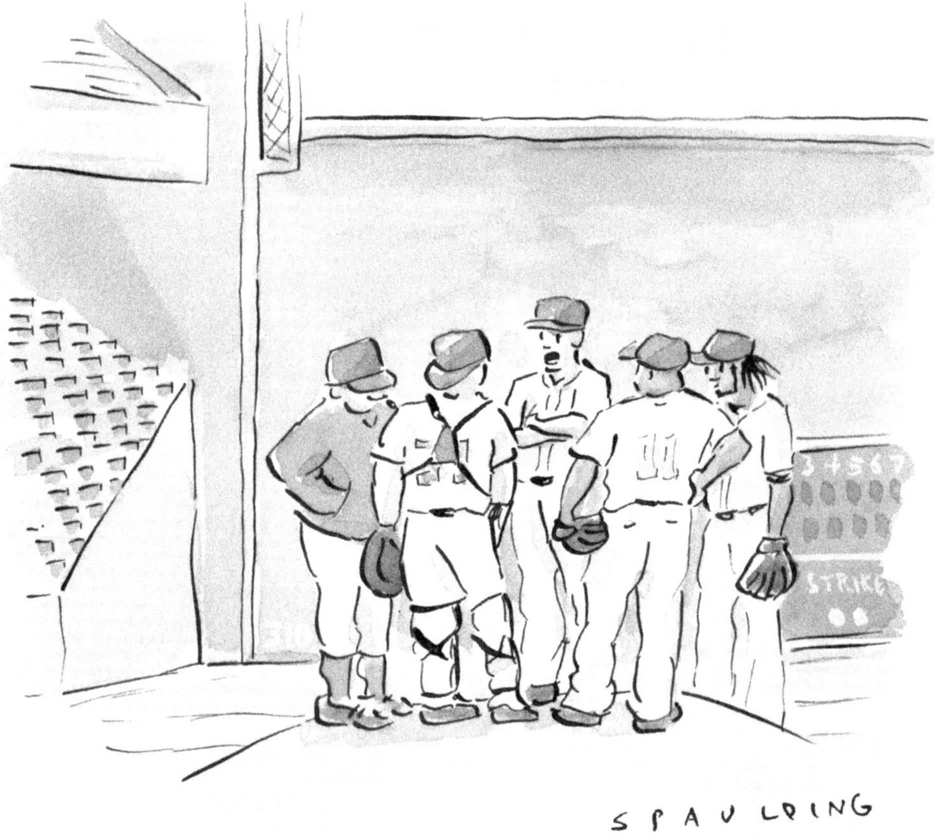
STRIKE
SPAULDING

"This could have just been an email."

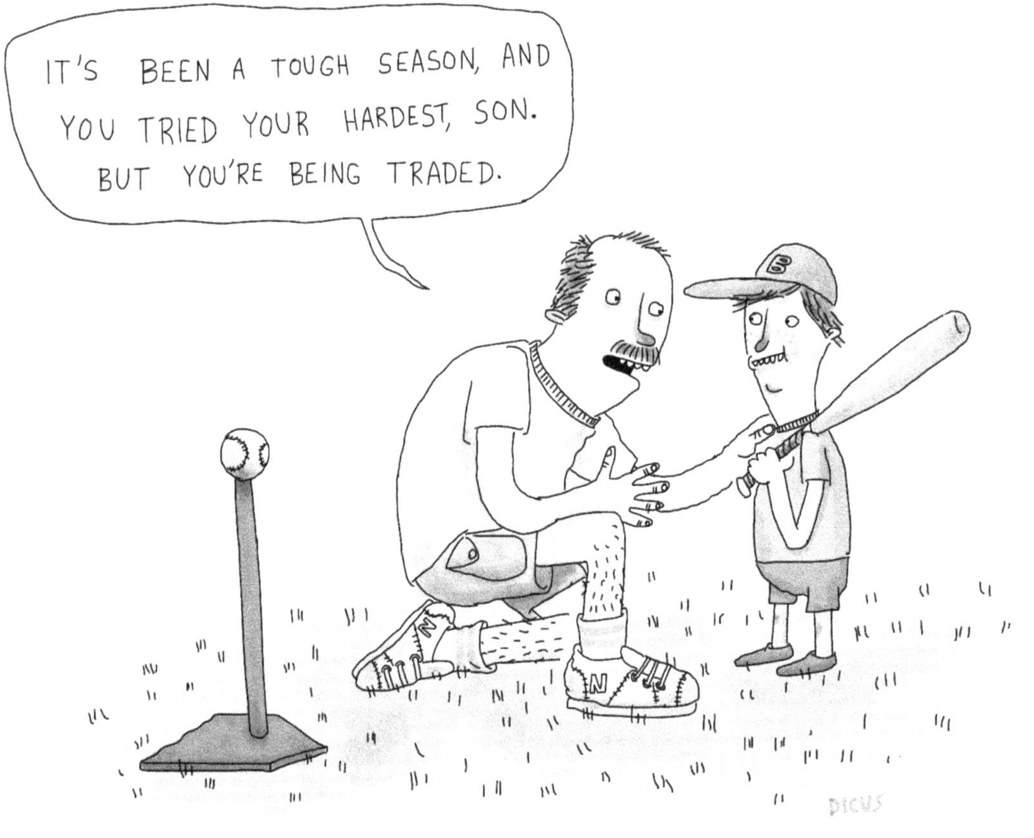
IT'S BEEN A TOUGH SEASON, AND YOU TRIED YOUR HARDEST, SON. BUT YOU'RE BEING TRADED.

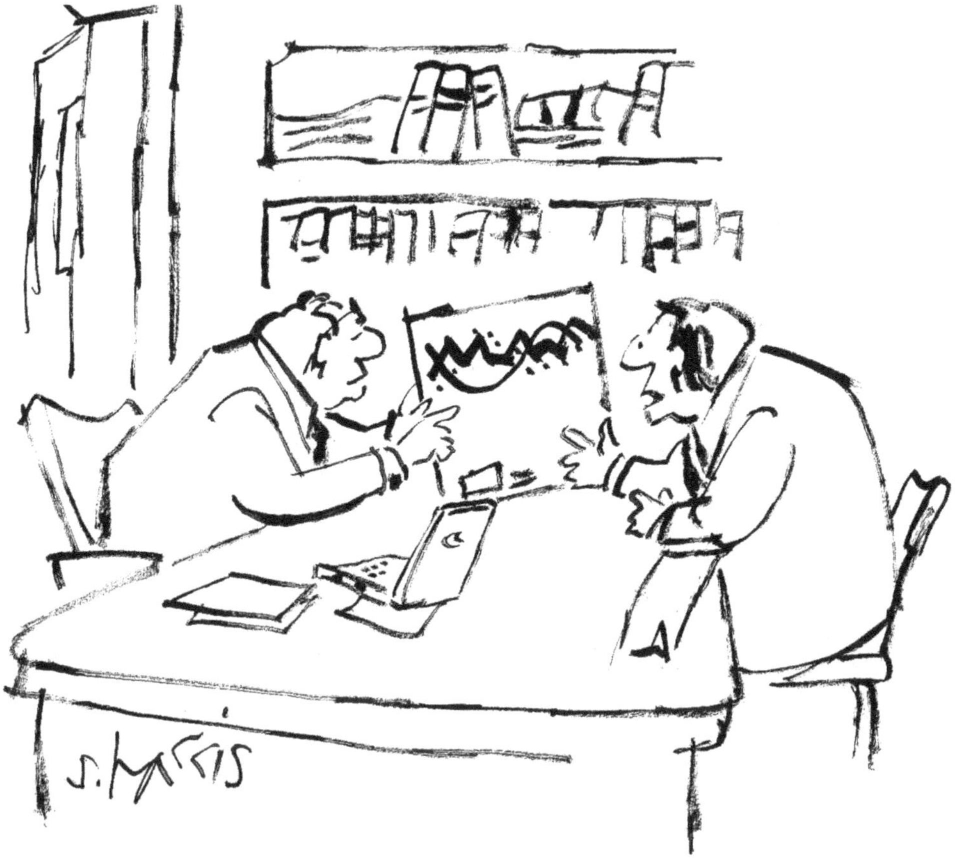
S. HARRIS

"I just don't see how an index fund tied to batting averages actually works."

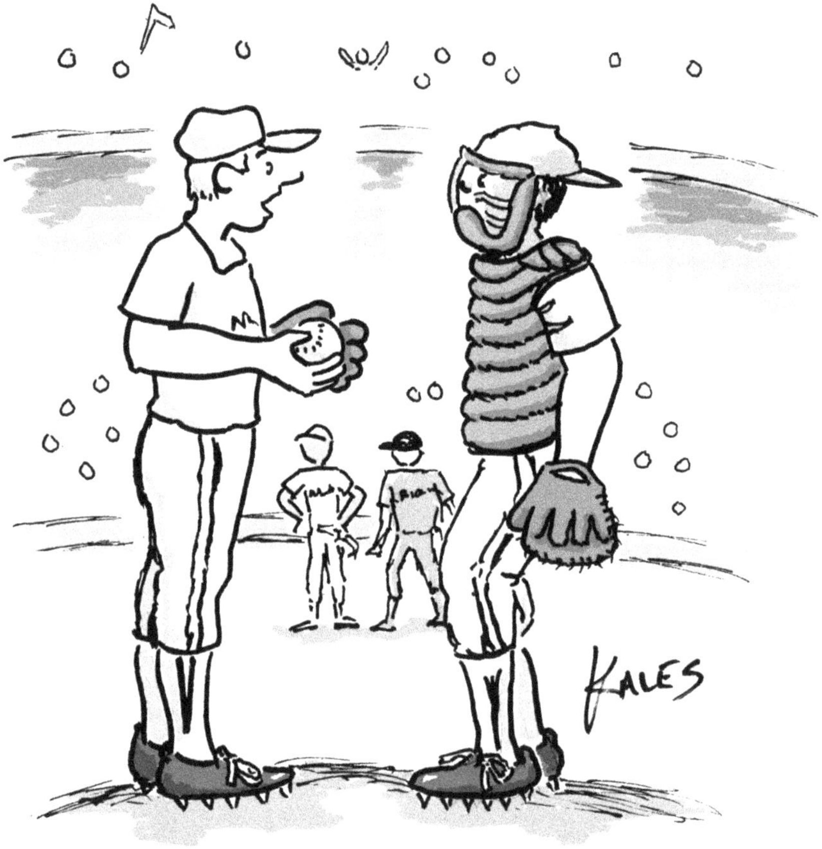
KALES

"For security, our signs need to be at least eight characters long."

THE END OF
MY FAVORITE
SERIES IS NEAR.

"Would you get me another beer? I have the express written consent of Major League Baseball."

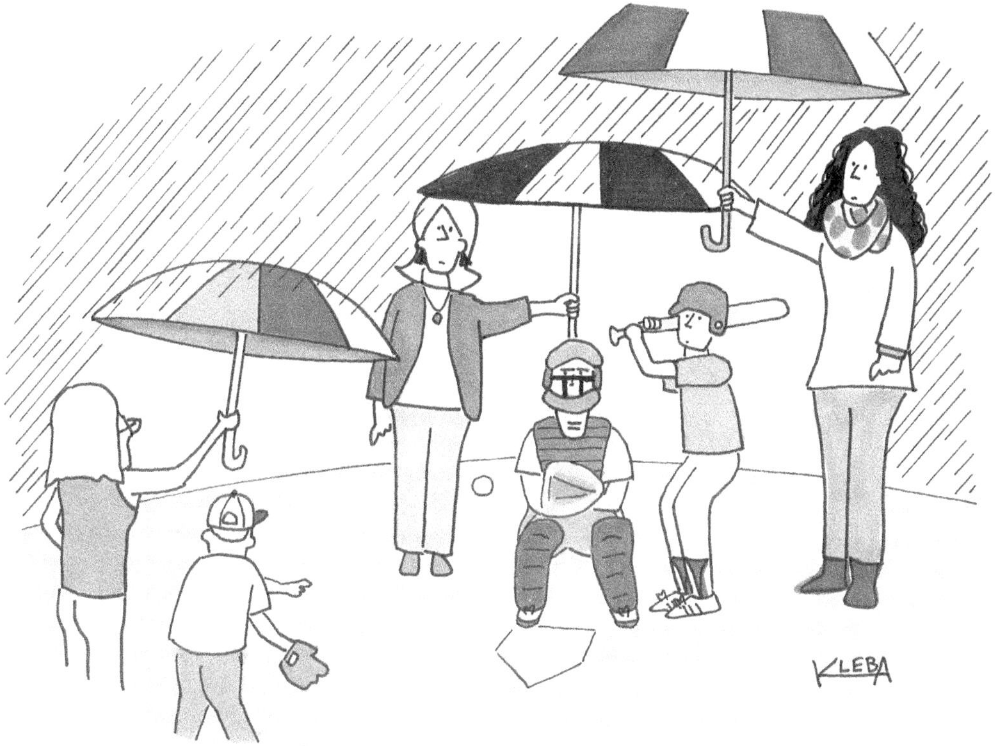
KLEBA

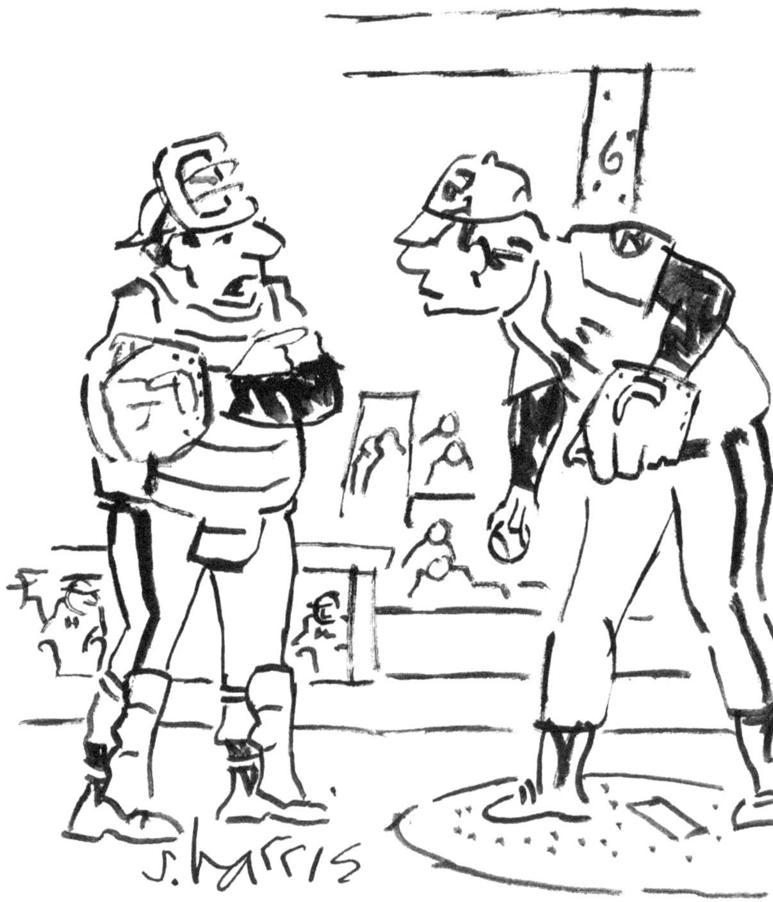
S. harris

*"All this pitching and hitting—
I'm convinced there's a deeper meaning to it all."*

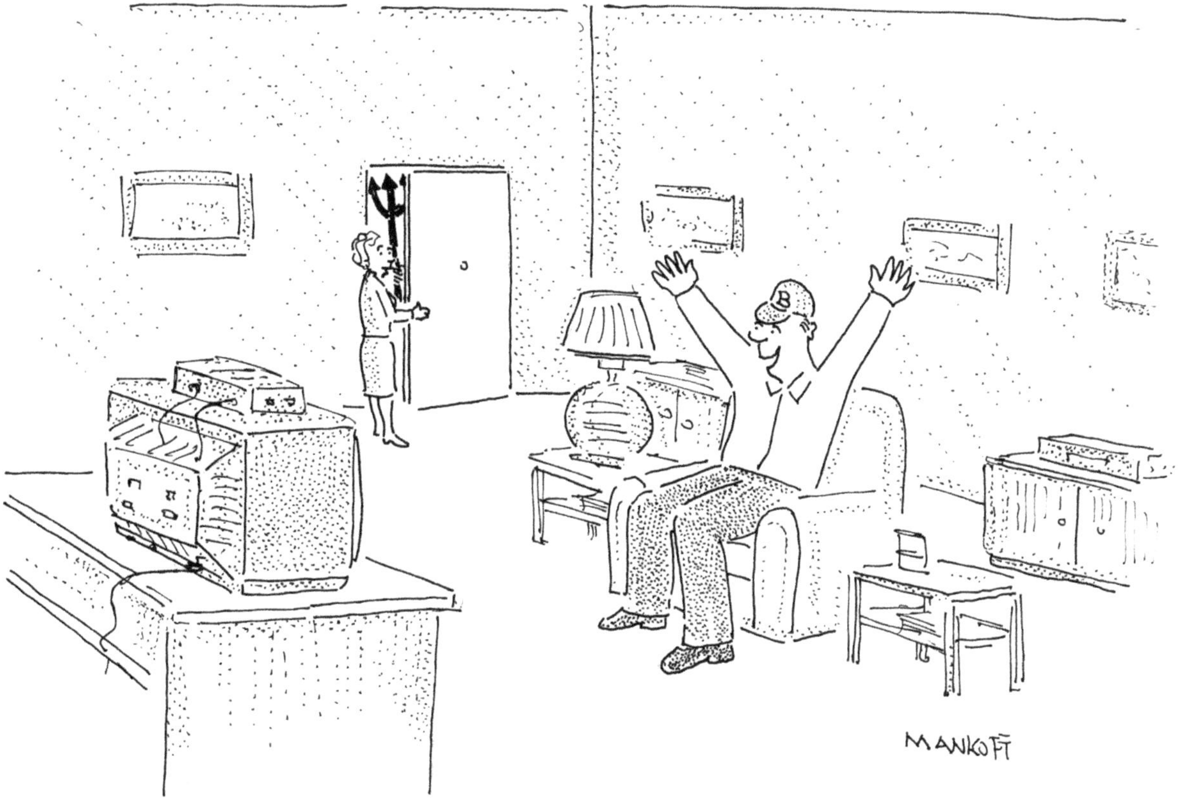
MANKOFF

"Dear, there's someone here to collect your soul."

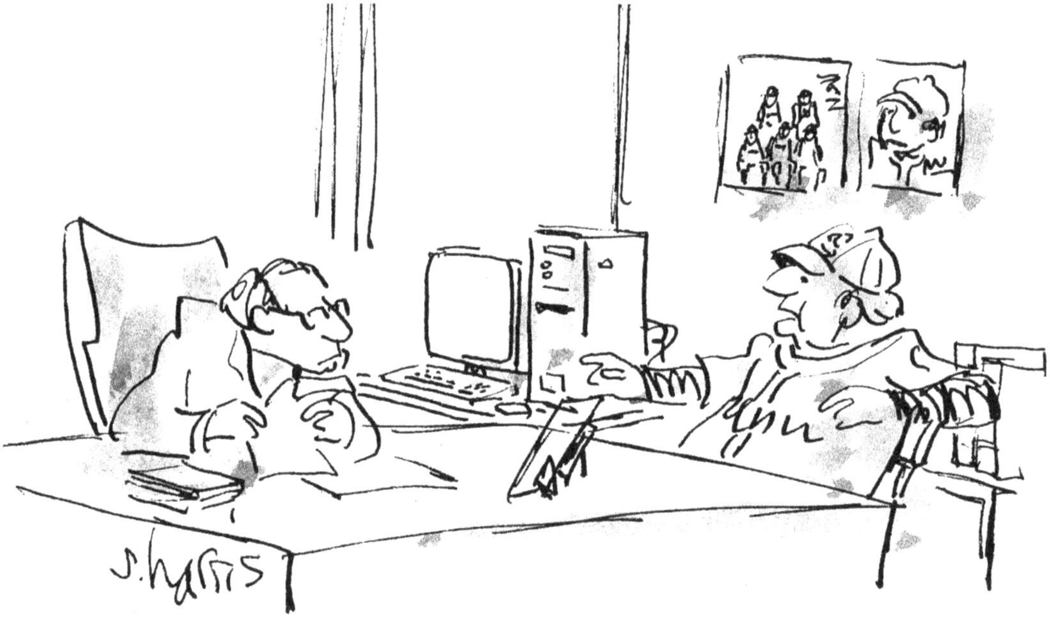
S.harris

*"I want the contract to say that if we win a championship of any sort,
no one spills champagne on my head."*

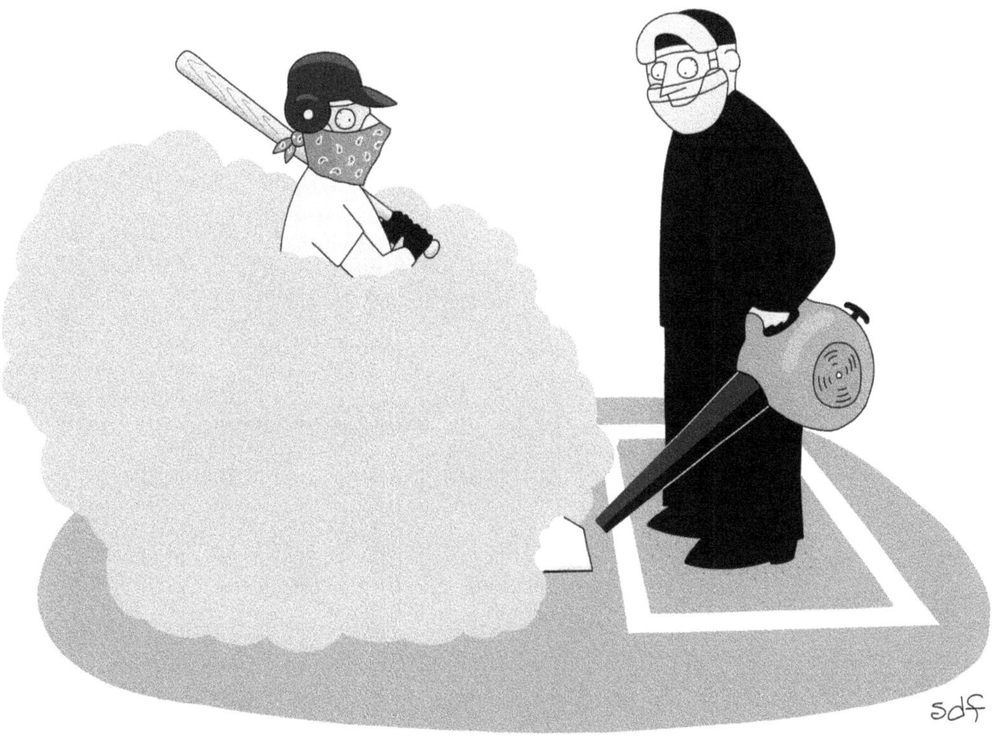
sdf

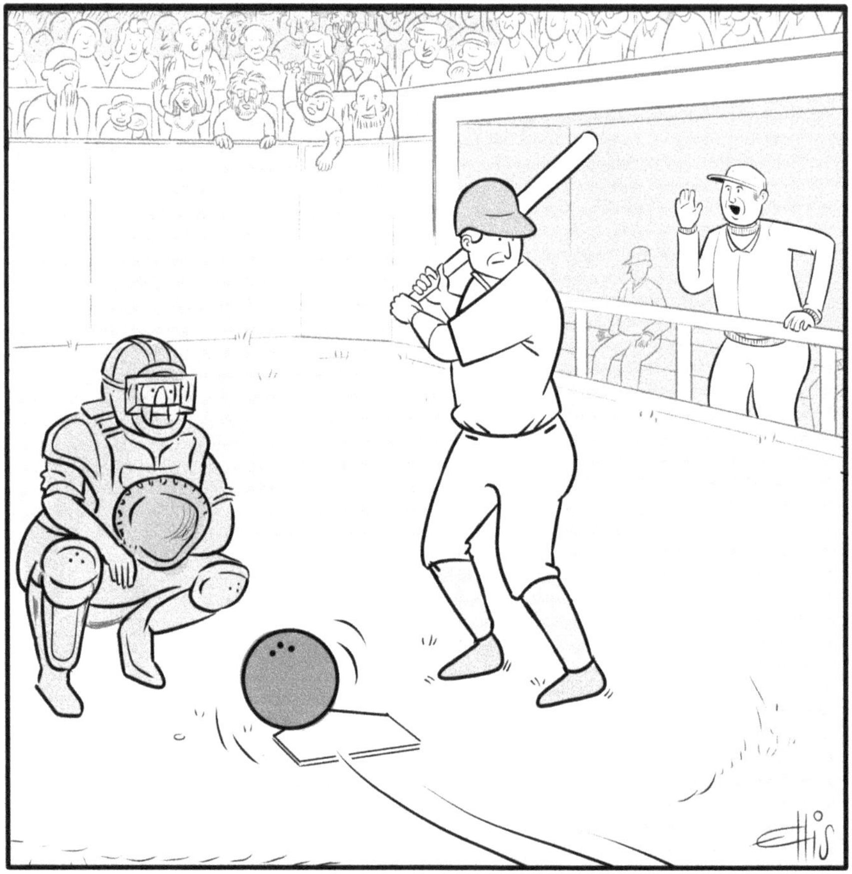
Ellis

"Good eye!"

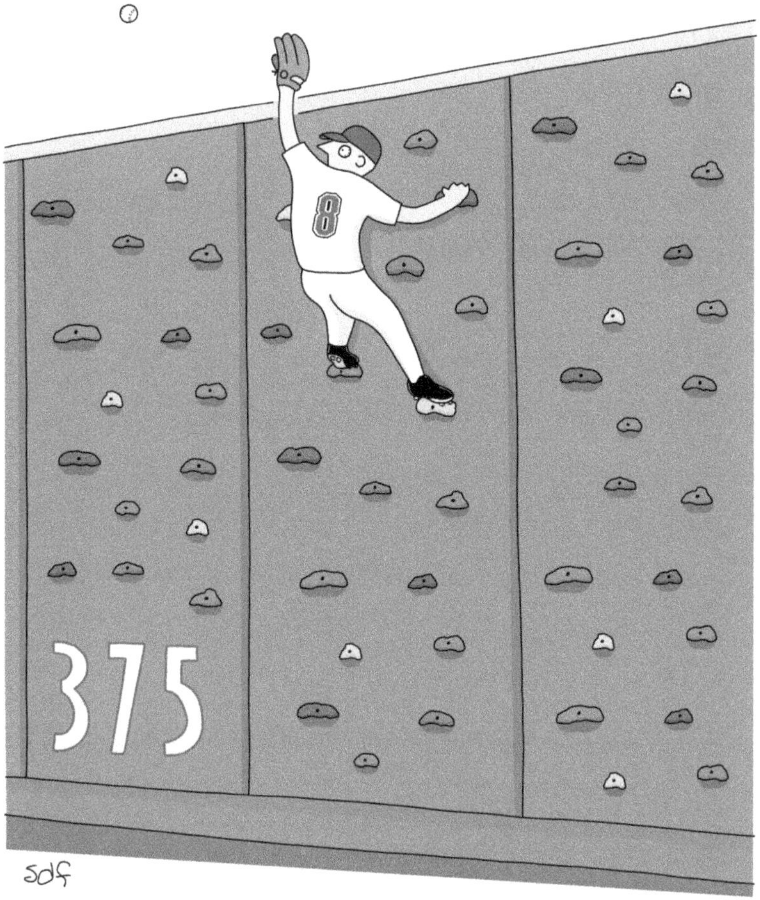
8
375
sdf

Index of Artists

www.ingramcontent.com/pod-product-compliance
Lightning Source LLC
Chambersburg PA
CBHW040847100426
42813CB00015B/2739